KU-363-096

COVID-19

We have re-checked every business in this book before publication to ensure that it is still open after the COVID-19 outbreak. However, the economic and social impacts of COVID-19 will continue to be felt long after the outbreak has been contained, and many businesses, services and events referenced in this guide may experience ongoing restrictions. Some businesses may be temporarily closed, have changed their opening hours and services, or require bookings; some unfortunately could have closed permanently. We suggest you check with venues before visiting for the latest information.

Top Experiences

Explore the Reichstag & Government Quarter

Germany's national political power nexus. **p40**

MATTHIAS MAKARINUS/GETTY IMAGES ©

Lonely planet

POCKET

BERLIN

TOP EXPERIENCES · LOCAL LIFE

ANDREA SCHULTE-PEEVERS

Contents

Plan Your Trip   4

Elephant Gate at Zoo Berlin (p110)
BORIS STROUJKO/SHUTTERSTOCK ©

Discover Treasures at the Pergamonmuseum

A cornucopia of ancient riches.
p60

Marvel at the Brandenburg Tor

Symbol of division and reunification.
p42

Catch an Exhibit at the Neues Museum
Spotlight on Egypt and Troy. **p64**

RADIOKAFKA/SHUTTERSTOCK ©

MICHELANGELOOP/SHUTTERSTOCK © ARCHITECTS: PETER EISENMAN

Learn at the Holocaust Memorial
Germany's central Holocaust memorial. **p44**

Explore Schloss Charlottenburg

Berlin's finest Prussian palace ensemble. **p120**

Take in History at the Gedenkstätte Berliner Mauer

Outdoor Berlin Wall memorial. **p94**

Wander Around Potsdamer Platz
Showcase of urban renewal. **p78**

ALEKSANDAR TODOROVIC/SHUTTERSTOCK © ARCHITECT: HELMUT JAHN

MICHELE RUZZI/SHUTTERSTOCK © ARCHITECT: DANIEL LIBESKIND

Experience History at the Jüdisches Museum
History of Jews in Berlin. **p56**

Walk Along the East Side Gallery

Berlin Wall vestige turned street-art gallery. **p146**

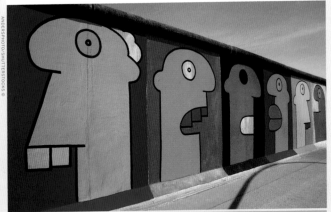

Discover Schloss & Park Sanssouci

Royal retreat amid landscaped gardens. **p170**

Dining Out

Berlin's food scene is growing in leaps and bounds, and maturing as beautifully as a fine Barolo. Sure, you can still get your fill of traditional German comfort staples, from sausage to roast pork knuckle, but it's the influx of innovative chefs from around the globe that makes eating in the capital such a mouth-watering experience.

Modern Regional Cuisine

Eating healthy while minimising your carbon footprint is sexy, which is why the organic-regional-seasonal trifecta has become an obsession in Berlin. Demand for regional ingredients is met by a growing number of farms in the surrounding state of Brandenburg. Some chefs even maintain their own vegetable and herb gardens or grow lettuce on-site in so-called 'vertical farms'.

Vegetarian & Vegan

A meal featuring meat is so last millennium, which is why vegan restaurants are spreading faster than rabbits on Viagra in Berlin. In 2018 Berlin's finest meat-free temple, Cookies Cream (p51), entered the pantheon of Michelin stars.

Local Snacks

A classic Berlin cult snack is the *Curry-wurst*, a fried or grilled *Wiener* sliced into bite-sized ringlets, swimming in a spicy tomato sauce and dusted with curry powder (pictured). The Berlin-style doner kebab, allegedly invented by a Turkish immigrant in 1970s West Berlin, features spit-roasted meat slivers tucked into a lightly toasted bread pocket along with salad and a healthy drizzle of yoghurt-based sauces.

Best German

Ora Regional-seasonal fare against the stylishly quaint backdrop of a 19th-century pharmacy. (p136)

GKRPHOTO/SHUTTERSTOCK ©

Orania.Restaurant Culinary magic from three ingredients per plate, plus the signature Xberg Duck. (p136)

Schwarzwaldstuben Oldies but goodies from Germany's south amid delightfully irreverent decor. (p103)

Best Vegan

Frea Zero-waste vegan pioneer in a Scandi-chic setting that has hip foodies in a headlock. (p101)

Kopps Vegan fine-dining trailblazer serving healthy, creative and gorgeous dishes. (p102)

1990 Vegan Living The bounty of Vietnamese meatless fare one small plate at a time. (p152)

Best Asian

Umami Sharp Indochine nosh for fans of the classics and the innovative. (p165)

Kin Dee Top Thai parlour for modern and localised spins on the classics. (p90)

Con Tho Trad recipes get a modern riff at this hip plant-based Vietnamese restaurant. (p134)

Best Middle Eastern

Malakeh Feistily flavoured Syrian soul food in a cosy lair with living-room flair. (p89)

Layla Middle Eastern dishes with global pizzazz. (p90)

Fes Turkish BBQ Grill your own meat and veg at this Turkish spin on Korean barbecue. (p136)

Top Tips

⊙ Reservations are essential at the top eateries and are recommended for midrange restaurants.

⊙ Your bill won't be presented until you ask for it: 'Zahlen, bitte.'

⊙ It's customary to add 10% or more for good service.

Bar Open

As one of Europe's primo party playgrounds, Berlin offers a thousand and one scenarios for getting your cocktails and kicks (or wine or beer, for that matter). From cocktail lairs and concept bars, craft beer pubs to rooftop lounges, the next thirst parlour is usually within stumbling distance.

Club Scene

What distinguishes the Berlin scene from other party capitals is a focus on independent, non-mainstream niche venues, run by owners or collectives with a creative rather than corporate background. The shared goal is to promote a diverse, inclusive and progressive club culture instead of maximising profit. Doors can be tough at top clubs, as staff strive to sift out those who might feel uncomfortable with the music, vibe or libertine ways past the door.

When to Go

Pubs are open from around noon to midnight or 1am (later on weekends). Trendy places and cocktail bars open around 7pm or 8pm and keep doors open until at least 2am and sometimes until the last tippler leaves. Clubs open at 11pm or midnight and start filling up around 1am or 2am.

Best Craft-Beer Pubs

Hopfenreich Berlin's first craft-beer bar also has tastings, tap takeovers and guest brewers. (p139)

BrewDog Trendy spot with 30 taps dispensing its own suds and guest draughts. (p168)

Hops & Barley Unfiltered pilsner, dark and wheat beer poured in a former butcher's shop. (p155)

Best Cocktail Bars

Buck & Breck Expertly prepared riffs on classics for grown-ups in a speakeasy-style setting. (p103)

Truffle Pig Follow the pig tracks through a corner pub to this clandestine drinking den. (p138)

Velvet Bar Seasonal potions created with imagination and unusual techniques. (p138)

TOMML/GETTY IMAGES ©

Zeroliq Sober bar where you can get your kicks with mocktails and alcohol-free beer and wine. (p154)

Best Beer Gardens

Rosengarten Enchanting rose garden with cold beers, cocktails and a cultural program. (p103)

Schleusenkrug Sprawling, classic joint sitting pretty next to a canal lock on the edge of the Tiergarten park. (p116)

Best Wine Bars

Otto Rink For relaxed but demanding wine fans with a penchant for German vintages. (p129)

Weinerei Forum Living-room flair with help-yourself and pay-what-you-like honour policy. (p167)

Best Rooftop Bars

Klunkerkranich Hipster spot with urban garden and great sunset views atop a Neukölln shopping centre. (p131)

Monkey Bar Trendy lair with exotic tiki drinks and a view of the baboons at Zoo Berlin. (p116)

Park Inn Panorama Terrasse Drinks at eye-level with the TV Tower in Berlin's tallest hotel. (p68)

Top Tips

○ Fancy labels and glam cocktail dresses can actually get in the way of your getting in. Wear something black, cool and casual.

○ Be respectful in the queue, don't drink and don't talk too loudly (seriously!). Don't arrive wasted.

Treasure Hunt

Berlin is a great place to shop, and we're definitely not talking malls and chains. The city's appetite for the individual manifests in small neighbourhood boutiques and buzzing markets that are a pleasure to explore. Shopping here is as much about visual stimulus as it is about actually spending your cash.

Where to Shop

Berlin's main shopping boulevard is Kurfürstendamm (Ku'damm) in the City West and Charlottenburg, which is largely the purview of mainstream retailers (from H&M to Prada). Its extension, Tauentzienstrasse, is anchored by KaDeWe, continental Europe's largest department store. Standouts among the city's dozens of other shopping centres are the concept mall Bikini Berlin and the vast LP12 Mall of Berlin at Leipziger Platz.

Getting the most out of shopping in Berlin, though, means venturing off the high street and into the *Kieze* (neighbourhoods). This is where you'll discover a cosmopolitan cocktail of indie boutiques stirred by the city's zest for life, envelope-pushing energy and entrepreneurial spirit.

Opening Hours

Malls, department stores and supermarkets open from 10am to 8pm or 9pm; some supermarkets are 24 hours. Boutiques and other smaller shops have flexible hours, usually from 11am to 7pm weekdays, and to 4pm or 5pm Saturday. Stores are closed on Sunday, except for some bakeries, flower shops, souvenir shops, and supermarkets in major train stations, including Hauptbahnhof, Friedrichstrasse and Ostbahnhof.

Best Shopping Areas

Kurfürstendamm Quintessential high-street shopping along with indie boutiques in the side streets. (p118)

MATYAS REHAK/SHUTTERSTOCK ©

Scheunenviertel Trendy local and international labels in chic boutiques and concept stores. (p105)

Kreuzberg & Neukölln Vintage fashion, eco-fashion, music and accessories, all in indie boutiques. (p140)

Flea Markets

Flohmarkt im Mauerpark The mother of all markets is overrun but still a good show. (pictured; p161)

Nowkoelln Flowmarkt International hipster market and showcase of local creativity. (p141)

Flohmarkt Boxhagener Platz Fun finds abound at this charmer on a leafy square. (p157)

Best Malls & Department Stores

Bikini Berlin Edgy shopping in a revitalised 1950s landmark building with hip concept stores and views of the monkeys at Zoo Berlin. (p118)

Mall of Berlin Huge high-end shopping quarter with 300 stores alongside apartments, a hotel and offices. (p91)

KaDeWe The largest department store in continental Europe. (p118)

Best Culinary Delights

KaDeWe Food Hall Mind-boggling bonanza of gourmet treats from around the world. (p118)

Markthalle Neun Revitalised historic market hall with thrice-weekly farmers market and global bites during Street Food Thursday. (p134)

Türkischer Markt Bazaar-like canal-side market with bargain-priced produce and Mediterranean deli fare. (p140)

Best One-of-a-Kind

Sugafari Take a trip around candy world at this sweet and colourful shop packed with global sugary treats. (p169)

Frau Tonis Parfum Bring home a fragrant memory of Berlin custom-mixed at this elegant perfume boutique. (p91)

Museums

With more museums than rainy days (around 170 at last count), Berlin has an extraordinarily diverse cultural landscape that caters for just about every interest, be it art, film, history, nature, computers or antiquities. Many of them are considered must-see attractions – and not just on rainy days.

Museum Island

Museum Island (Museumsinsel), a Unesco World Heritage site, presents 6000 years of art and cultural history in five massive repositories. Marvel at antiquities at the Pergamonmuseum and Altes Museum, meet Egyptian queen Nefertiti at the Neues Museum, take in 19th-century art at the Alte Nationalgalerie and admire medieval sculptures at the Bode-Museum.

History Museums

From its humble medieval beginnings, Berlin's history – and especially its key role in major events of the 20th century – is a rich and endlessly fascinating tapestry. It's also extremely well documented, in numerous museums, memorial sites and monuments, many of them in original historic locations and most of them free.

Nationalgalerie Berlin

The National Gallery is a top-ranked collection of mostly European art from the 19th century to today. The Alte Nationalgalerie (p68) specialises in neoclassical, romantic, impressionist and early modernist art; at the Hamburger Bahnhof (p98) the spotlight is on international contemporary art; the Museum Berggruen (p122) focuses on Picasso; the Sammlung Scharf-Gerstenberg (p122) on surrealist art; and the **Friedrich-swerdersche Kirche** on 19th-century sculpture.

Best History Museums

Deutsches Historisches Museum Comprehensive journey through 1500 years of Germany's turbulent past. (p48)

JAMES BEDFORD/LONELY PLANET ©

Jüdisches Museum Goes beyond the Holocaust in tracing the history of Jews in Germany. (p56)

DDR Museum Engaging look at daily life behind the Iron Curtain. (pictured; p67)

Best for Antiquities

Pergamonmuseum Treasure trove of monumental architecture from ancient civilisations. (p60)

Altes Museum Gorgeous Schinkel building sheltering priceless antique art and sculpture. (p67)

Neues Museum Pay your respects to Egyptian queen Nefertiti and her entourage. (p64)

Best Niche Museums

Bröhan Museum Beautiful objects and furniture from the art deco, art nouveau and functionalist periods. (p122)

Museum für Naturkunde Meet giant dinos in Berlin's own 'Jurassic Park'. (p98)

Museum für Film und Fernsehen An entertaining romp through German celluloid history. (p79)

Worth a Trip

The original Checkpoint Charlie guard cabin, a Berlin Airlift plane and a reconstructed spy tunnel are among the exhibits at the **Allied Museum** (☑030-818 1990; www.alliiertenmuseum.de; Clayallee 135; admission free; ☺10am-6pm Tue-Sun; Ⓟ; ☐115, X83, ⓊOskar-Helene-Heim), which documents historic events and the challenges faced by the Western Allies during the Cold War. It's in the southwestern suburb of Grunewald.

Architecture

After visiting the German capital in 1891, Mark Twain remarked, 'Berlin is the newest city I've ever seen'. True then, still true now. Destruction and division have ensured that today's city is essentially a creation of modern times, a showcase of 20th-century styles with few surviving vestiges of earlier times.

Post-Reunification

The fall of the Wall in 1989 presented Berlin with both the challenge and the opportunity to redefine itself architecturally. Huge gashes of empty space opened where the city's halves were to be rejoined. The grandest of the developments is Potsdamer Platz, a contemporary interpretation of the famous historic square. Other standouts include the Bundeskanzleramt (Federal Chancellery), the Jüdisches Museum and the Neues Museum.

The Schinkel Touch

The architectural style that most shaped Berlin was neoclassicism, thanks in large part to one man: Karl Friedrich Schinkel (1781–1841), arguably Prussia's most prominent architect. His first solo commission was the Neue Wache, but the nearby Altes Museum is considered his most mature work.

The 1920s & Bauhaus

The spirit of innovation brought some of the finest avant-garde architects to Berlin in the 1920s, including Le Corbusier, Ludwig Mies van der Rohe and Hans Scharoun. Their association later evolved into the Bauhaus, which used practical anti-elitist principles to unite form and function and had a profound effect on modern aesthetics.

Best of Schinkel

Altes Museum The grand colonnaded front inspired by a philosophers school in Athens is considered Schinkel's most mature work. (p67)

Konzerthaus Berlin A sweeping staircase leads to a raised columned portico

ANYAIVANOVA/SHUTTERSTOCK ©

in this famous concert hall. (pictured; p54)

Neue Wache This royal guardhouse turned antiwar memorial was Schinkel's first Berlin commission. (p50)

architectural metaphor for Jewish history. (p56)

Neues Museum David Chipperfield's reconstructed New Museum ingeniously blends old and new. (p64)

Sony Center Helmut Jahn's svelte glass-and-steel complex is the most striking building on Potsdamer Platz. (p79)

Best Post-WWII Modernism

Berliner Philharmonie This eccentric concert hall is Hans Scharoun's modernist masterpiece. (p91)

Haus der Kulturen der Welt Avant-garde structure with gravity-defying sculptural roof. (p48)

Best Contemporary

Jüdisches Museum Daniel Libeskind's zigzag-shaped

Worth a Trip

Built for the 1936 Olympic Games, Berlin's coliseum-style **Olympiastadion** (Olympic Stadium; ☎030-2500 2322; https://olympia stadion.berlin; Olympischer Platz 3; adult/ concession self-guided tour €8/5.50, tours from €11/9.50; ⏰9am-7pm Apr-Jul, Sep & Oct, to 8pm Aug, 10am-4pm Nov-Mar; 🅿; Ⓢ Olympiastadion, Ⓤ Olympiastadion) was revamped for the 2006 FIFA World Cup and now sports a spidery oval roof, snazzy VIP boxes, and top sound, lighting and projection systems.

Historical Sites

In Berlin the past is always present. Strolling along boulevards and around neighbourhoods, you can't help but pass legendary sights that take you back to the era of Prussian glory, the dark ages of the Third Reich, the tense period of the Cold War and the euphoria of reunification.

The Age of Prussia

Berlin has been a royal residence since 1701 when Elector Friedrich III elevated himself to King Friedrich I. This promotion significantly shaped the city, which blossomed under Frederick the Great, who sought greatness as much on the battlefield as through building. In the 19th century, Prussia weathered revolutions and industrialisation to forge the creation of the German Reich, which lasted until the monarchy's demise in 1918.

The Third Reich

No other political power shaped the 20th century as much as Nazi Germany. The megalomania of Hitler and his henchmen wrought destruction upon much of Europe, bringing death to at least 50 million people, and forever realigned the world order. Few original sites remain, but memorials and museums make sure the horror is not forgotten.

Cold Wall Chills

After WWII, Germany fell into the crosshairs of the Cold War as a country divided along ideological lines by the victorious powers, its internal border marked by fences and a wall. Just how differently the two countries developed is still palpable in Berlin, expressed not only through Berlin Wall remnants such as the East Side Gallery but also through vastly different urban planning and architectural styles.

Best of Prussian Pomp

Brandenburger Tor Germany's most iconic national symbol. (p42)

NICHOLASGERALDINEPHOTOS/SHUTTERSTOCK ©

Schloss Charlottenburg
Sumptuous palace providing a glimpse into the lifestyles of the rich and royal. (p120)

Berliner Dom Royal court church with impressive dimensions, stunning acoustics and fanciful sarcophagi. (pictured; p67)

Best of Cold War Berlin

Gedenkstätte Berliner Mauer Exhibit illustrating the history, physical appearance and social impact of the Berlin Wall. (p94)

East Side Gallery The longest remaining stretch of Berlin Wall turned street art canvas by more than 100 artists. (p146)

Karl-Marx-Allee East Berlin's pompous yet impressive main boulevard and showpiece of socialist architecture. (p150)

Best of WWII History

Topographie des Terrors Gripping examination of the origins of Nazism, its perpetrators and its victims, on the site of the SS and Gestapo headquarters. (p85)

Holocaust Memorial Commemorates the unspeakable horrors of the WWII Jewish genocide. (p44)

Worth a Trip

In January 1942 high-ranking Nazi officials gathered on Lake Wannsee in southwestern Berlin to hammer out details of the systematic deportation and murder of European Jews: the 'Final Solution'. A 13-room exhibit documents the sinister meeting in what is now the **Haus der Wannsee-Konferenz** (☑030-805 0010; www.ghwk.de; Am Grossen Wannsee 56-58; admission free; ◷10am-6pm; Ⓢ Wannsee, then bus 114).

Art

Art aficionados will find their compass on perpetual spin in Berlin. Home to hundreds of galleries, scores of world-class collections and some 20,000 professional artists, it has assumed a pole position on the global artistic circuit.

Commercial Art Galleries

The **Galleries Association of Berlin** (www. berliner-galerien.de) counts some 340 galleries within the city. In addition, there are at least 200 noncommercial showrooms and off-spaces that regularly show new exhibitions. Although the orientation is global, it's well worth keeping an eye out for the latest works by major contemporary artists living and working in Berlin, including Thomas Demand, Jonathan Meese, Via Lewandowsky, Isa Genzken, Tino Sehgal, Esra Ersen, John Bock, and the artist duo Ingar Dragset and Michael Elmgreen.

Galleries cluster in four main areas: along Auguststrasse and Linienstrasse in the Scheunenviertel; around Checkpoint Charlie (eg Zimmerstrasse, Markgrafenstrasse); on Potsdamer Strasse in Schöneberg; and around Savignyplatz near Kurfürstendamm.

Public Art

Free installations, sculptures and paintings? Absolutely.

Public art is big in Berlin, which happens to be home to the world's longest outdoor mural, the 1.3km-long East Side Gallery (p146). No matter which neighbourhood you walk in, you're going to encounter public art on a grand scale.

Best Old Masters

Gemäldegalerie Sweeping survey of six centuries of canvas candy from Germany, Italy, France, Spain and the Netherlands. (p74)

Alte Nationalgalerie Showcase of 19th-century art by leading German romantics and realists. (p68)

ANDERSPHOTO/SHUTTERSTOCK ©

Best Niche Collections

Museum Berggruen Priceless Picassos, plus works by Klee and Giacometti. (p122)

Sammlung Scharf-Gerstenberg Enter the surreal worlds conjured up by Goya, Max Ernst, Magritte and other giants of the genre. (p122)

Best Contemporary Art

Hamburger Bahnhof Legends like Warhol, Beuys and Twombly are aboard at this former train station. (p98)

Sammlung Boros Book months ahead for tickets to see this cutting-edge private collection in a WWII bunker. (pictured; p98)

Best Street Art

Urban Nation Museum Presents a changing roster of the best street artists in a modernised 19th-century building. (p125)

Haus Schwarzenberg Awesome works on courtyard facades of this hub of subculture. (p100)

RAW Gelände Constantly evolving canvas with dedicated street-art gallery called Urban Spree. (p156)

Worth a Trip

For some of the best street art in town, head to the abandoned US **spy station** (www.teufelsberg-berlin.de; Teufelschaussee; tickets €5, with photo permission €10, tours €15; ⏱11am-sunset Wed-Sun, last entry 1hr before sunset; Ⓢ Heerstrasse) crowning the Teufelsberg, a 121.1m-high hill built from wartime debris in the Grunewald forest. The derelict compound also offers mesmerising all-round views of Berlin.

Tours

If you're a Berlin first-timer, letting someone else show you around is a great way to get your bearings, see the key sights quickly and obtain a general understanding of the city. All manner of explorations – from generic city bus tours to special-interest outings – are available.

Walking & Cycling Tours

Several companies offer English-language general city explorations and themed tours (eg Third Reich, Cold War, Potsdam). Tickets are sold online but some don't require reservations – you just show up at the designated meeting point. Some guides work for tips only so give generously. Most tours cost between €15 and €25 and run three or four hours.

Boat Tours

On a warm day, it's fun to see Berlin from the deck of a boat cruising the city's rivers, canals and lakes. Tours range from one-hour spins around the historic centre to longer trips to Schloss Charlottenburg. Operators provide commentary in English and German and sell refreshments on board. Embarkation points cluster around Museum Island; check the website of **Stern + Kreis** (☏030-536 3600; www.sternund kreis.de; tours from €17; ◷Mar-Dec) for other locations.

Best Cycling & Walking Tours

Alternative Berlin Tours (☏0162 819 8264; www.alternativeberlin. com; tours €14-35) Roster includes tip-based general tours, a street-art tour (with optional workshop) and a nightlife tour.

Berlin on Bike (☏030-4373 9999; www.berlinon bike.de; Knaackstrasse 97, Kulturbrauerei, Court 4; tours incl bike adult/ concession €29/25, bike rental per 24hr €10-15; ◷8am-8pm mid-Mar–mid-Nov, 10am-4pm Mon-Fri mid-Nov–mid-Mar; ⛎M1, ⓊEberswalder Strasse) Daily city and Berlin Wall tours along with Alternative Berlin and Street Art tours.

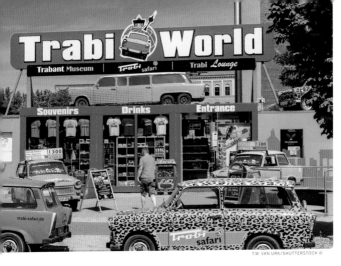

T.W. VAN URK/SHUTTERSTOCK ©

Original Berlin Walks

(📞 0177 302 9194; www.
berlinwalks.de; adult/conces-
sion from €20/18) Berlin's
longest-running English-
language walking tour company has a large roster of
general and themed tours.

Best Speciality
Tours

Berliner Unterwelten

(📞 030-4991 0517; www.
berliner-unterwelten.
de; Brunnenstrasse 105;
adult/concession €12/10;
🕑 hours vary; **S** Gesundbrunnen, **U** Gesundbrunnen)
Get a look at Berlin from
below as you explore a dark
and dank subterranean
WWII air-raid shelter.

Refugee Voices Tours

(📞 0157 5221 5445; www.
refugeevoicestours.org;
🕑 by request) Learn about
Berlin from the perspective
of a Syrian refugee on walks
around the central area.

Eat the World (📞 030-
206 229 990; www.eat-
the-world.com; tours adult
weekday/weekend €29/39,
child €20) Berlin one bite
at a time on three-hour
culinary sightseeing tours
with stops at cafes, delis,
bakeries and more.

Trabi Safari (pictured;
📞 030-3020 1030; www.
trabi-safari.de; Zimmer-
strasse 97; adult/child
under 18yr from €49/free;
🕑 ticket shop 10am-5pm;
U Kochstrasse) Turn the
clock back while driving
yourself around the city in
an original East German
Trabant car.

Top
Tip

Get a crash course in 'Berlin-ology' by
hopping on public bus 100 or 200 at
Zoologischer Garten or Alexanderplatz
and letting the sights whoosh by for
the price of an AB transport ticket. Also
handy: bus 300, which goes from Potsdamer Platz to the East Side Gallery.

LGBTIQ+

Berlin's legendary liberalism has spawned one of the world's biggest, most divine and diverse LGBTIQ+ playgrounds. Anything goes in 'Homopolis' (and we do mean anything!), from the highbrow to the hands-on, the bourgeois to the bizarre, the mainstream to the flamboyant.

Community

The area around Nollendorfplatz (Motzstrasse and Fuggerstrasse especially) has been a gay mecca since the 1920s. Institutions like Heile Welt, Tom's, Connection and Hafen pull in the punters night after night, and there's also plenty of nocturnal action for the leather and fetish set. The crowd skews younger, wilder and more alternative around Kottbusser Tor and along Oranienstrasse, where key venues stay open till sunrise and beyond. For a DIY subcultural vibe, head across the canal to Neukölln. Things are comparatively subdued in the bars and cafes along main-strip Mehringdamm. Friedrichshain is a de rigueur stop on the gay nightlife circuit thanks to clubs like Berghain, the hands-on Lab.oratory, Suicide Circus and :// about blank.

Partying

Generally speaking, Berlin's gayscape runs the entire spectrum from mellow cafes, campy bars and cinemas to saunas, cruising areas, clubs with darkrooms and all-out sex venues. In fact, sex and sexuality are entirely everyday matters to the unshockable city folks. As elsewhere, gay men have more options for having fun, but women, trans and other genders don't have to feel left out.

Note that most clubs and parties are on hiatus because of the COVID-19 pandemic. However, some organisers have found ways to keep going while meeting social distancing requirements, eg by moving the party outdoors.

SERGEY KOHL/SHUTTERSTOCK ©

Best Bars

Heile Welt (📞030-2191 7507; www.facebook.com/heileweltbar; Motzstrasse 5; ⏱7pm-3am; Ⓤ Nollendorfplatz) Stylish lounge good for chatting and mingling over cocktails.

Zum Schmutzigen Hobby (📞030-3646 8446; www.facebook.com/zumschmutzigenhobby; RAW Gelände, Revaler Strasse 99, Gate 2; ⏱6pm-late; 🚋M10, M13, Ⓢ Warschauer Strasse, Ⓤ Warschauer Strasse) Fabulously wacky party pen in a former fire station.

Himmelreich (📞030-2936 9292; www.himmelreich-berlin.de; Simon-Dach-Strasse 36; ⏱5pm-2am or later Mon-Sat, 4pm-1am or later Sun; 🚋M13, M10, Ⓢ Warschauer Strasse, Ⓤ Warschauer Strasse) Fifties retro lounge that's a lesbigay-scene stalwart in Friedrichshain.

Rauschgold (📞030-9227 4178; www.rauschgold.berlin; Mehringdamm 62; ⏱from 8pm; 🛜; Ⓤ Mehringdamm) Glitter-glam bar for all-night fun with pop, karaoke and drag shows.

Sally Bowles (📞030-2083 8269; www.sally-bowles.de; Eisenacher Strasse 2; ⏱6pm-1am Tue-Sun; 🚋M19, M29, Ⓤ Nollendorfplatz) Classy cafe-bar with a neighbourhood vibe and delightful 1920s decor.

Best Sights

Schwules Museum (Gay Museum; 📞030-6959 9050; www.schwulesmuseum.de; Lützowstrasse 73; adult/concession €9/3; ⏱2-6pm Mon, Wed, Fri & Sun, to 8pm Thu, to 7pm Sat; 🚋M29, 100, Ⓤ Nollendorfplatz, Kurfürstenstrasse) Dive deep into the history of queer Berlin through exhibits, events and extensive archives.

Denkmal für die im Nationalsozialismus verfolgten Homosexuellen (Memorial to the Persecuted Homosexuals under National Socialism; www.stiftung-denkmal.de; Ebertstrasse; admission free; ⏱24hr; Ⓢ Brandenburger Tor, Potsdamer Platz, Ⓤ Brandenburger Tor, Potsdamer Platz) Memorial to the suffering of Europe's LGBTIQ+ community under the Nazis; on Ebertstrasse on the edge of Tiergarten park.

Under the Radar

Berlin is a multifaceted metropolis that is constantly in flux. There's always something new and exciting to discover, so help keep overtourism in check by going beyond the top blockbuster sights in the city centre and connecting with local life and key sights in Berlin's outer boroughs.

RIADSEIF/SHUTTERSTOCK ©

Gärten der Welt
(pictured; Gardens of the World; ☏030-700 906 720; www.gaertenderwelt.de/en/; Blumberger Damm 44; adult/child €7/free Mar-Oct, €4/free Nov-Feb,; ☉9am-sunset; P; U Kienberg-Gärten der Welt) Travel the world one garden at a time surrounded by Berlin's largest prefab housing development.

Zitadelle Spandau
(Spandau Citadel; ☏030-354 9440; www.zitadelle-berlin.de; Am Juliusturm 64; adult/concession €4.50/2.50, audioguide €2; ☉10am-5pm Fri-Wed, 1-8pm Thu, last entry 30min before closing; U Zitadelle) Play hide and seek in Europe's largest Renaissance military fortress, complete with moat, drawbridge and arrowhead-shaped bastions.

Deutsch-Russisches Museum (German-Russian Museum Berlin-Karlshorst; ☏030-5015 0810; www.museum-karlshorst.de; Zwieseler Strasse 4; admission free; ☉10am-6pm Tue-Sun; S Karlshorst) Stand in the spot where Nazi Germany's WWII capitulation was signed.

Brücke-Museum (☏030-831 2029; www.bruecke-museum.de; Bussardsteig 9; adult/concession/under 18yr €6/4/free, with Kunsthaus Dahlem €8/5/free; ☉11am-5pm Wed-Mon; P; U Oskar-Helene-Heim, then bus 115 or X10 to Pücklerstrasse) Admire the vivid Expressionist canvasses painted by members of Die Brücke (The Bridge), Germany's first modern-art group, between 1905 and 1913.

Pfaueninsel (Peacock Island; ☏0331-969 4200; www.spsg.de; Nikolskoer Weg; return ferry adult/child €4/3; ☉ferry 10am-6pm Apr-Oct, to 4pm Nov-Mar; S Wannsee, then bus 218) Get romantic on this enchanting island in the Havel River with roaming peacocks and a snowy-white fairy-tale palace built for royal hanky-panky.

Haus der Wannsee-Konferenz (☏030-805 0010; www.ghwk.de; Am Grossen Wannsee 56-58; admission free; ☉10am-6pm; S Wannsee, then bus 114) Visit stately villa on Lake Wannsee where Nazi officials hammered out the details of the 'Final Solution': the systematic deportation and murder of European Jews.

For Kids

Travelling to Berlin with kids can be child's play, especially if you keep a light schedule and involve them in day-to-day planning. There's plenty to do to keep youngsters occupied, from zoos – the Zoo Berlin being the most popular – to kid-oriented museums. Parks and imaginative playgrounds abound in all neighbourhoods, as do public pools.

ANTICICLO/SHUTTERSTOCK ©

Legoland Discovery Centre (pictured; ☎01806-6669 0110; www.legoland discoverycentre.de/berlin; Potsdamer Strasse 4; €19.50; ☺10am-7pm Wed-Sun, last admission 5pm; ☒200, 300, M41, ⑤Potsdamer Platz, ⓤPotsdamer Platz) The milk-tooth set delights in this Lego wonderland with rides, entertainment and interactive stations.

Deutsches Technikmuseum (German Museum of Technology; ☎030-902 540; https://technikmuseum.berlin; Trebbiner Strasse 9; adult/concession/child under 18yr €8/4/after 3pm free; ☺9am-5.30pm Tue-Fri, 10am-6pm Sat & Sun, last entry 4pm; Ⓟ♿; ⓤGleisdreieck, Möckernbrücke) This vast shrine to technology is packed

with discoveries, including the world's first computer, an entire hall of vintage locomotives, and exhibits on aerospace and navigation in a modern annexe.

Science Center Spectrum (☎030-9025 4284; https://technikmuseum.berlin/spectrum; Möckernstrasse 26; adult/concession/child under 18yr €8/4/free after 3pm; ☺9am-5.30pm Tue-Fri, 10am-6pm Sat & Sun, last entry 4pm; Ⓟ; ⓤMöckernbrücke, Gleisdreieck) Play with, experience and learn about such things as balance, weight, water, air and electricity in dozens of hands-on science experiments.

Tierpark Berlin (☎030-515 310; www.tierpark-berlin.de; Am Tierpark 125;

adult/concession/child 4-15yr €14.50/9.50/7; ☺zoo 9am-6.30pm Apr-Sep, to 6pm Mar & Oct, to 4.30pm Nov-Feb, palace 1-5pm Thu-Sat year-round; Ⓟ♿; ⓤTierpark) Expect plenty of ooh and aah moments when kids watch baby elephants at play or see lions and tigers being fed at this vast animal park.

Sealife Berlin (☎0180-666 690 101; www.visitsea life.com; Spandauer Strasse 3; adult/child €19/15; ☺10am-6pm, last admission 5pm; ☒100, 200, 245, ⑤Hackescher Markt, Alexanderplatz) Little ones get to press their noses against dozens of fish-filled tanks, solve puzzles and admire starfish and sea anemones up close.

Four Perfect Days

Day 1

ROMAN SIGAEV/SHUTTERSTOCK ©

One day in Berlin? Check off the key sights on this whirl-wind itinerary. Book ahead for access to the **Reichstag** (p40) dome, then snap a picture of the **Brandenburg Gate** (p42) before exploring the **Holocaust Memorial** (p44) and admiring the contemporary architecture of **Potsdamer Platz** (p78).

Head to **Checkpoint Charlie** (pictured; p85) and saunter over to glorious **Gendarmenmarkt** (p48) square and lunch at **Galeries Lafayette** (p55). Head east and pop into the brand-new **Humboldt Forum** (p69) culture centre and the antiquities-filled **Pergamonmuseum** (p60).

Wind down on a **river cruise**, book ahead for dinner at **Frea** (p101) and wrap up with cocktails at **Buck & Breck** (p103).

Day 2

M DOGAN/SHUTTERSTOCK ©

Start the day by coming to grips with life in Berlin when the Wall still stood at the **Gedenk-stätte Berliner Mauer** (p94). Poke around the boutiques on Kastanienallee before grabbing lunch at **W-Der Imbiss** (p165).

Stroll down to the Scheunenvi-ertel to explore the **Hackesche Höfe** (p98) and the **New Synagogue** (pictured; p99) before enjoying a coffee-and-cake break at riverside **Petit Bijou** (p61) with a view of the ornate Bode-Museum.

Head to Kreuzberg for dinner at **Orania** (p136), then follow up with a bar-hop around Kottbusser Tor, pulling up for cocktails at **Würgeengel** (p129), beer at **Möbel Olfe** (p129) or wine at **Otto Rink** (p129).

Day 3

KIRSTYLEEISZ/SHUTTERSTOCK ©

Kick the day off at **Schloss Charlottenburg** (p120), where the **Neuer Flügel** (New Wing) is an essential stop. Meditate upon the futility of war at the **Kaiser-Wilhelm-Gedächtniskirche** (p110), then – assuming it's not Sunday – satisfy your shopping cravings along **Kurfürstendamm** capped by lunch in the **KaDeWe** (p118) food hall.

Swing by the striking Daniel Libeskind–designed **Jüdisches Museum** (p56), then head down to **Tempelhofer Feld** (pictured; p143) to see how an old airport can be recycled into a sustainable park and playground.

Wrap up the day with dinner at **eins44** (p138) followed by a bar-hop along **Weserstrasse** and side streets.

Day 4

MICHAEL KAERCHER/SHUTTERSTOCK ©

Leave the city bustle behind on a saunter around the parks and royal palaces in Potsdam. Book time-slot online tickets for **Schloss Sanssouci** (p171), a rococo jewel of a palace, then explore the surrounding park and its many smaller palaces, including the exotic **Chinesisches Haus** (p103).

Head into Potsdam's old town for a spin around the **Holländisches Viertel** (Dutch Quarter; pictured) or marvel at top-notch art in the dashing **Museum Barberini** (p105) before heading back to Berlin to wind down at the enchanting **Rosengarten** (p103) beer garden.

For dinner pull up a stool at Prenzlauer Berg's buzzy **Umami** (p165) for modern Vietnamese fare, then head to **Bryk Bar** (p168) for a nightcap.

Need to Know

For detailed information, see Survival Guide (p175)

Currency
Euro (€)

Language
German

Visas
Generally not required for tourist stays of up to 90 days; some nationalities need a Schengen visa.

Money
Credit cards are widely accepted and ATMs ubiquitous.

Mobile Phones
Mobile phones operate on GSM900/1800. Local SIM cards can be used in unlocked multiband phones.

Time
Central European time (GMT/UTC plus one hour)

Tipping
Servers 10%, bartenders 5%, taxi drivers 10%, porters €1 to €2 per bag, room cleaners €1 to €2 per day, toilet attendants €0.50.

Daily Budget

Budget: Less than €100
Dorm bed or peer-to-peer rental: €18–35
Doner kebab: €3–4
Club cover: €5–20
Public transport day pass: €8.60

Midrange: €100–200
Private apartment or double room: €80–120
Two-course dinner with wine: €40–60
Guided public tour: €10–20
Museum admission: €8–30

Top end: More than €200
Upmarket apartment or double in top-end hotel: from €180
Gourmet two-course dinner with wine: €80
Cabaret ticket: €50–80
Taxi ride: €25

Advance Planning

Two to three months before Book tickets for the Berliner Philharmonie, the Staatsoper, Sammlung Boros and top-flight events.

One month before Reserve a table at trendy or Michelin-starred restaurants, especially for Friday and Saturday dinners.

Two weeks before Book online tickets for the Reichstag dome, the Neues Museum and the Pergamonmuseum (summer only).

Arriving in Berlin

✈ Berlin Brandenburg Airport

FEX Airport Express trains twice hourly (30 minutes); RE7 and RE14 trains hourly (30 minutes); S9 trains every 20 minutes (45 minutes). All train journeys €3.60. Taxi to city centre €60.

🚊 Hauptbahnhof

Main train station in the city centre near government district; served by S-Bahn, U-Bahn, tram, bus and taxi.

🚌 Zentraler Omnibus Bahnhof (ZOB)

The central bus station is on the western city-centre edge. U-Bahn U2 to city centre (eg Zoo station, eight minutes; Alexanderplatz, 28 minutes), €2.90; taxi €15 to City West, €28 to Alexanderplatz.

Getting Around

U U-Bahn

Most efficient way to travel; operates 4am to 12.30am and all night Friday, Saturday and public holidays. From Sunday to Thursday, half-hourly night buses take over.

S S-Bahn

Less frequent than U-Bahn trains but with fewer stops; useful for longer distances. Same operating hours as the U-Bahn.

🚌 Bus

Slow but useful for sightseeing on the cheap. Run frequently 4.30am to 12.30am; half-hourly night buses in the interim. MetroBuses (designated eg M1, M19) operate 24/7.

🚋 Tram

Only in the eastern districts; MetroTrams (designated eg M1, M2) run 24/7.

Berlin Neighbourhoods

Hackescher Markt & Scheunenviertel (p93)
The maze-like historic Jewish Quarter is fashionista central and also teems with hip bars and restaurants.

Schloss Charlottenburg

Kurfürstendamm & City West (p107)
Nirvana for shopaholics, this grand boulevard spills into idyllic side streets flanked by chic boutiques and bustling cafes and restaurants.

Reichstag

Brandenburger Tor

Hol Men

Gemäldegalerie

Potsdamer Platz

Potsdamer Platz (p73)
Built in the 1990s on ground once bisected by the Berlin Wall, this quarter is a showcase of fabulous contemporary architecture.

Reichstag & Unter den Linden (p39)
Berlin's historic hub delivers great views, iconic landmarks and the city's most beautiful boulevard.

Prenzlauer Berg (p159)
This charismatic neighbourhood entices with fun shopping, gorgeous townhouses, cosy cafes and a fabulous flea market.

Gedenkstätte Berliner Mauer

Pergamonmuseum

Neues Museum

ocaust morial

Museum Island & Alexanderplatz (p59)
Gawk at a pirate's chest of treasure from ancient civilisations guarded by the soaring TV Tower on socialist-styled Alexanderplatz.

East Side Gallery

Kreuzberg & Neukölln (p127)
Gritty but cool, Kreuzberg and Neukölln are a joy to explore on foot, with vibrant restaurant scenes and Berlin's most happening nightlife.

Friedrichshain (p145)
This gentrifying district sports high-profile GDR-era relics, rambunctious nightlife and eclectic shopping.

Explore
Berlin

Worth a Trip 👀

City's Walking Tours 🥾

Berliner Dom (p67) ANDREY OMELYANCHUK/500PX ©

Explore ⊛
Reichstag &
Unter den Linden

It's been burned, bombed, rebuilt, buttressed by the Berlin Wall, wrapped in fabric and, finally, adorned with a glass dome: the iconic Reichstag, seat of the German parliament (Bundestag). Nearby, the Brandenburg Gate gives way to the stately Pariser Platz square and Unter den Linden, Berlin's most elegant boulevard, which flaunts its Prussian pedigree with pride.

The Short List

○ **Reichstag (p40)** *Standing in awe of history at Germany's parliament building, then pinpointing the sights while meandering up its landmark glass dome.*

○ **Brandenburger Tor (p42)** *Snapping a selfie with this famous landmark and symbol of German reunification.*

○ **Gendarmenmarkt (p48)** *Taking in the architectural symmetry of this gorgeous square.*

○ **Holocaust Memorial (p44)** *Soaking in the presence of uncounted souls before gaining insight into the horrors of the Holocaust.*

Getting There & Around

🚌 Lines 100, 245 and 300 run along most of Unter den Linden.

Ⓢ S1 and S2/25 stop at Brandenburger Tor and Friedrichstrasse.

Ⓤ Stadtmitte (U2, U6), Unter den Linden (U5, U6) and Hausvogteiplatz (U2) are convenient for Gendarmenmarkt.

Neighbourhood Map on p46

Reichstag (p40) WESTEND61/GETTY IMAGES © ARCHITECT: NORMAN FOSTER

Top Experience 📷

Explore the Reichstag & Government Quarter

The federal government quarter snuggles neatly into the Spreebogen, a horseshoe-shaped bend in the Spree River. Its historic anchor is the glass-domed Reichstag, which once rubbed against the western side of the Berlin Wall. It now forms part of a row of modern government buildings that symbolically link the former East and West Berlin across the Spree.

◉ MAP P46, C2

☎ 030-2273 2152

www.bundestag.de

admission free

🕑 lift 8am–midnight, last entry 9.45pm

🚌 100, Ⓢ Brandenburger Tor, Ⓤ Brandenburger Tor, Bundestag

Reichstag Building

The four corner towers and mighty facade with the bronze dedication 'Dem Deutschen Volke' (To the German People; added in 1916) are the only original sections of the 1894 Reichstag. Norman Foster, the architectural mastermind of the building's post-reunification modernisation, preserved the historical shell and added the sparkling glass dome. The original dome, made of steel and glass and considered a high-tech marvel at the time, was destroyed during the Reichstag fire in 1933.

Reichstag Dome

Whoever said the best things in life are free might have been thinking of the lift ride up to the rooftop of the Reichstag. Enjoy the knockout views, then pick up a free audioguide and learn about the building, Berlin landmarks and the workings of the Bundestag while following the ramp up and around the dome's mirror-clad funnel.

Bundeskanzleramt

The Federal Chancellery, Germany's 'White House', is a sparkling, modern compound designed by Axel Schultes and Charlotte Frank, and consists of two parallel office blocks flanking a central white cube. Eduardo Chillida's rusted-steel *Berlin* sculpture graces the forecourt.

Paul-Löbe-Haus

The glass-and-concrete Paul-Löbe-Haus houses offices for the Bundestag's parliamentary committees. A double footbridge links it to the Marie-Elisabeth-Lüders-Haus across the Spree in a visual symbol of reunification.

Marie-Elisabeth-Lüders-Haus

Home to the parliamentary library, this extravagant structure has a massive tapered stairway, a jutting roofline and giant circular windows. In the basement is an **art installation** by Ben Wagin featuring original segments of the Berlin Wall.

★ Top Tips

o Free advance reservations for visiting the Reichstag dome must be made online at www.bundestag.de. Bring picture ID.

o Without reservations, swing by the **Reichstag Visitors' Centre** (☎030-2273 2152; www.bundestag.de; Scheidemannstrasse; ☺8am-8pm Apr-Oct, to 6pm Nov-Mar; 🚌100, Ⓢ Brandenburger Tor, Ⓤ Bundestag) to enquire about last-minute openings.

o Free multilingual guides are available on the roof terrace.

✕ Take a Break

o Book at least two weeks ahead for a table at the Dachgartenrestaurant Käfer (p52) on the Reichstag rooftop.

o For snacks and beer, report to the **Restaurant Populär** (☎030-2065 4737; www.berlin-pavillon.de; Scheidemannstrasse 1; dishes €4.50-9; ☺8am-9pm), a Frisbee toss away at the edge of Tiergarten park.

Top Experience 📷

Marvel at the Brandenburger Tor

Brandenburg Gate is Berlin's most famous – and most photographed – landmark. Trapped right behind the Berlin Wall during the Cold War, it went from symbol of division to epitomising German reunification when the hated barrier fell in 1989. It now serves as a photogenic backdrop for raucous New Year's Eve parties, concerts, festivals and mega-events including FIFA World Cup finals.

◎ MAP P46, D3

Brandenburg Gate

Pariser Platz

Ⓢ Brandenburger Tor,
Ⓤ Brandenburger Tor

Origins

Commissioned by Prussian king Friedrich Wilhelm II, the gate was completed in 1791 as a symbol of peace and a suitably impressive entrance to the grand boulevard Unter den Linden. Architect Carl Gotthard Langhans looked to the Acropolis in Athens for inspiration for this elegant triumphal arch, which is the only surviving one of 18 city gates that once ringed historical Berlin.

Architecture

Standing 26m high, 65.5m wide and 11m deep, the neoclassical sandstone gate is fronted by 12 Doric columns and divided into five passageways. The wider central passage was reserved for the king and his entourage; common folk had to use the four narrower ones.

Quadriga

Crowning the Brandenburg Gate is the *Quadriga*, Johann Gottfried Schadow's famous sculpture of a winged goddess piloting a chariot drawn by four horses. After trouncing Prussia in 1806, Napoleon kidnapped the lady and held her hostage in Paris until a gallant Prussian general freed her in 1815. Afterwards, the goddess was equipped with a triumphal iron cross wrapped in an oak wreath and topped with a Prussian eagle.

Pariser Platz

Completely flattened in WWII, this once elegant square spent the Cold War trapped just east of the Berlin Wall. Look around now: the US, French and British embassies, banks and a luxury hotel have returned to their original sites and once again frame the bustling plaza, just as they did during its 19th-century heyday.

★ Top Tips

o If you need a moment of peace and quiet, visit the *Raum der Stille* (Room of Silence) in the gate's northern wing.

o There is a tourist office in the southern wing.

o The gate is at its most photogenic early in the morning and at sunset.

✕ Take a Break

o The **Art Canteen** (☎030-200 571 723; www.art-canteen.de; Pariser Platz 4; dishes €7-10; ⏰11am-5pm Tue-Fri) bistro inside the Akademie der Künste serves refreshments, vegan and omni lunches and build-your-own bowls.

o For a stylish break, enjoy coffee or champagne next to the elephant fountain in the lobby of the venerable **Hotel Adlon Kempinski** (☎030-226 10; www. kempinski.com; Unter den Linden 77, Pariser Platz; r from €320; ⓅⓈ❄🏊🐾).

Top Experience 📷

Learn at the Holocaust Memorial

The **Denkmal für die ermordeten Juden Europas** *(Memorial to the Murdered Jews of Europas) was officially dedicated in 2005. Colloquially known as the Holocaust Memorial, it's Germany's central memorial to the Nazi-planned genocide during the Third Reich. For the football-field-sized space, New York architect Peter Eisenman created 2711 sarcophagus-like concrete stelae (slabs) of various heights, rising from the undulating ground.*

◎ MAP P46, D4

📞 030-263 9430

www.stiftung-denkmal.de

Cora-Berliner-Strasse 1

audioguide €3

🕐 24hr

Ⓢ Brandenburger Tor,
Ⓤ Brandenburger Tor

Field of Stelae

You're free to access this massive concrete maze at any point and make your individual journey through it. At first it may seem austere, even sterile. But take time to feel the coolness of the stone and contemplate the interplay of light and shadow, then stumble aimlessly among the narrow passageways, and you'll soon connect with a metaphorical sense of disorientation, confusion and claustrophobia.

Ort der Information

For context, visit the subterranean Ort der Information, which movingly lifts the veil of anonymity from the six million Holocaust victims. A graphic timeline of Jewish persecution during the Third Reich is followed by a series of rooms documenting the fates of individuals and families. The most visceral is the darkened **Room of Names**, where the names and years of birth and death of Jewish victims are projected onto all four walls while a solemn voice reads their short biographies. Poignant and heart-wrenching, these exhibits will leave no one untouched. Not recommended for children under 14.

Gay Memorial

Europe's LGBTIQ+ community suffered enormously under the Nazis, as is commemorated by this free-standing, 4m-high, off-kilter concrete cube designed by Michael Elmgreen and Ingar Dragset. A looped video plays through a warped, narrow window. It's off Ebertstrasse, on the edge of Tiergarten.

Roma & Sinti Memorial

This memorial by Dani Karavan commemorates the Sinti and Roma victims of the Holocaust and consists of a circular reflecting pool with a floating stone decorated daily with a fresh flower. It's in the Tiergarten, just north of the Brandenburger Tor.

★ Top Tips

o For a more in-depth experience, rent an audioguide (€3).

o Free one-hour guided tours in English run at 11am on Friday, Saturday and Sunday.

o The memorial is at its moodiest (and most photogenic) when shadows are long, ie early morning or late in the day.

✕ Take a Break

o If you like it hot, head to Liu Nudelhaus (p50) for its Sichuan Zajiang noodle dish.

o Lots of eating and drinking options, including healthy dishes at Ki-Nova (p89), are a short stroll south at Potsdamer Platz.

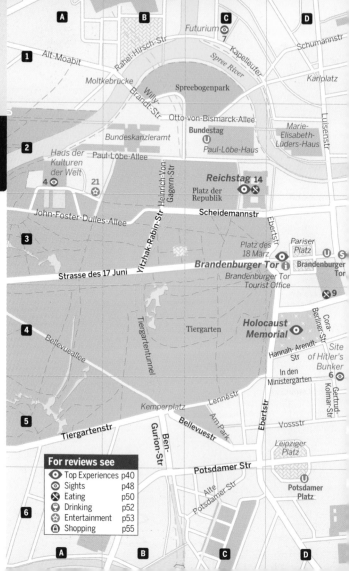

A **B** **C** **D**

1

Alt-Moabit

Rahel-Hirsch-Str

Futurium ⊙
7

Kapelleufer-

Schumannstr

Spree River

Karlplatz

Moltkebrücke

Willy-

Spreebogenpark

Brandt-Str

Otto-von-Bismarck-Allee

2

Bundeskanzleramt

Bundestag
Ⓤ
Paul-Löbe-Haus

Marie-
Elisabeth-
Lüders-Haus

Luisenstr

Haus der
Kulturen
der Welt

Paul-Löbe-Allee

4 ⊙

21
★

Reichstag 14
⊙ ✕
Platz der
Republik

John-Foster-Dulles-Allee

Heinrich-Von-

Gagern-Str

Scheidemannstr

Ebertstr

3

Yitzhak-Rabin-Str

Platz des
18 März ⊙

Pariser
Platz

Ⓤ Ⓢ

Brandenburger Tor ℹ

Brandenburger
Tor

Strasse des 17 Juni

Brandenburger Tor
Tourist Office

✕ 9

Cora-
Berliner-Str

4

Bellevueallee

Tiergartentunnel

Tiergarten

Holocaust
Memorial ⊙

Hannah-Arendt-
Str

In den
Ministergärten

Site
of Hitler's
Bunker
6 ⊙

Gertrud-
Kolmar-Str

Lennéstr

5

Kemperplatz

Bellevuestr

Am Park

Ebertstr

Vossstr

Tiergartenstr

Ben-
Gurion-Str

Leipziger
Platz

Potsdamer Str

Ⓤ
Potsdamer
Platz

Alte
Potsdamer Str

6

For reviews see	
⊙ Top Experiences	p40
⊙ Sights	p48
✕ Eating	p50
🍺 Drinking	p52
★ Entertainment	p53
🔒 Shopping	p55

A **B** **C** **D**

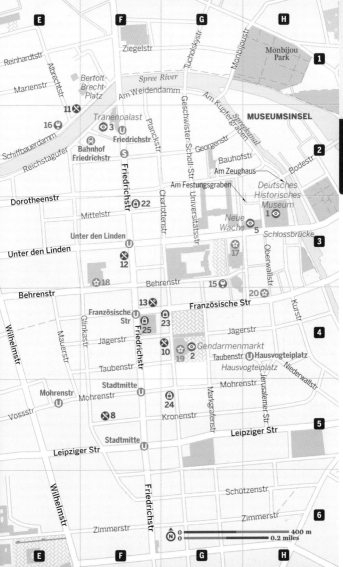

Reichstag & Unter den Linden

E · F · G · H

1
Reinhardtstr
Marienstr
Ziegelstr
Monbijou Park

Bertolt-Brecht-Platz
Albrechtstr
Spree River
Am Weidendamm

MUSEUMSINSEL

11
16 🚇
Tranenpalast
3 🔵 🚇
Friedrichstr
Bahnhof Friedrichstr Ⓢ
Schiffbauerdamm
Reichstagufer

Geschwister-Scholl-Str
Tucholskystr
Monbijoustr
Am Kupfergraben
Georgenstr
Spreekanal
Bauhofstr
Bodestr

2

Dorotheenstr
Mittelstr
🚇 22
Friedrichstr
Charlottenstr
Universitätsstr
Am Festungsgraben
Am Zeughaus
Deutsches Historisches Museum
1 🔵

3

Unter den Linden
🚇
Unter den Linden
12 ✖
18 ⭐
Behrenstr
Neue Wache
5 🔵
Schlossbrücke
17 ⭐
15 🚇
Oberwallstr

Behrenstr
20 ⭐
Kurstr

4

Wilhelmstr
Mauerstr
Glinkastr
13 ✖
Französische Str 🚇
Französische Str
23 🔒
25 🔵
Jägerstr
10 ✖
19 ⭐ 2 🔵 *Gendarmenmarkt*
Taubenstr 🚇 **Hausvogteiplatz**
Hausvogteiplatz
Niederwallstr
Jerusalemer Str

5

Vossstr
Mohrenstr 🚇
Stadtmitte 🚇
Mohrenstr
24 🔒
✖ 8
Kronenstr
Markgrafenstr
Mohrenstr
Leipziger Str

Leipziger Str
Stadtmitte 🚇
Friedrichstr
Schützenstr

6

Zimmerstr
Ⓝ 0 _____ 400 m
0 _____ 0.2 miles
Zimmerstr

E · F · G · H

Sights

Deutsches Historisches Museum
MUSEUM

1 MAP P46, H3

If you're wondering what Germans have been up to for the past 1500 years, take a spin around the baroque Zeughaus, formerly the Prussian arsenal and now home of the German Historical Museum. Upstairs, displays concentrate on the period from the 6th century to the end of WWI in 1918, while the ground floor tracks the 20th century all the way through to the fall of the Berlin Wall. An audioguide is available (€3). (German Historical Museum; ☎030-203 040; www.dhm.de; Unter den Linden 2; permanent exhibit free, IM Pei Bau adult/concession/under 18yr €8/4/free; ☺10am-6pm; 🚌100, 245, 300, Ⓤ Hausvogteiplatz, Ⓢ Hackescher Markt)

Gendarmenmarkt
SQUARE

2 MAP P46, G4

This graceful square is bookended by two domed churches and punctuated by a grandly porticoed concert hall, the Konzerthaus (p54). It was named for the Gens d'Armes, an 18th-century Prussian regiment consisting of French Huguenot refugee soldiers. (Ⓤ Französische Strasse, Stadtmitte)

Tränenpalast
MUSEUM

3 MAP P46, F2

During the Cold War, tears flowed copiously in this glass-and-steel border-crossing pavilion where East Berliners had to bid adieu to family visiting from West Germany – hence its 'Palace of Tears' moniker. The exhibit uses original objects (including the claustrophobic passport-control booths and a border auto-firing system), photographs and historical footage to document the division's social impact on the daily lives of Germans on both sides of the border. (☎030-467 777 911; www.hdg.de; Reichstagufer 17; admission free; ☺9am-7pm Tue-Fri, 10am-6pm Sat & Sun; 🚌M1, 12, Ⓢ Friedrichstrasse, Ⓤ Friedrichstrasse)

Haus der Kulturen der Welt
NOTABLE BUILDING

4 MAP P46, A2

This highly respected cultural centre showcases contemporary non-European art, music, dance, literature, films and theatre, and also serves as a discussion forum on zeitgeist-reflecting issues. The gravity-defying parabolic roof of Hugh Stubbins' extravagant building, designed as the American contribution to a 1957 architectural exhibition, is echoed by Henry Moore's sculpture *Butterfly* in the reflecting pool. (House of World Cultures; ☎030-397 870; www.hkw.de; John-Foster-Dulles-Allee 10; admission varies; ☺exhibits noon-8pm Wed-Mon; Ⓟ; 🚌100, Ⓢ Hauptbahnhof, Ⓤ Bundestag, Hauptbahnhof)

Berlin under the Swastika

The rise to power of Adolf Hitler and the NSDAP (Nazi Party) in January 1933 had instant and far-reaching consequences for all of Germany. Within three months, all non-Nazi parties, organisations and labour unions had been outlawed and many political opponents, intellectuals and artists detained without trial. Jews, of course, were a main target from the start but the horror escalated for them during the Kristallnacht pogroms on 9 November 1938, when Nazi thugs desecrated, burned and demolished synagogues and Jewish cemeteries, property and businesses across the country. Jews had begun to emigrate after 1933, but this event set off a stampede.

The fate of those Jews who stayed behind is well known: their systematic, bureaucratic and meticulously documented annihilation in death camps, mostly in Nazi-occupied territories in Eastern Europe. Sinti and Roma (gypsies), political opponents, priests, gays, people with disabilities and habitual criminals were targeted as well. Of the roughly seven million people who were sent to concentration camps, only 500,000 survived.

The Battle of Berlin

With the Normandy invasion of June 1944, Allied troops arrived in formidable force on the European mainland, supported by unrelenting air raids on Berlin and most other German cities. The final Battle of Berlin began in mid-April 1945, with 1.5 million Soviet troops barrelling towards the city from the east. On 30 April, when the fighting reached the government quarter, Hitler and his long-time companion Eva Braun killed themselves in their bunker. As their bodies were burning, Red Army soldiers raised the Soviet flag above the Reichstag.

Defeat & Aftermath

The Battle of Berlin ended on 2 May, with Germany's unconditional surrender six days later. The fighting had taken an enormous toll on Berlin and its people. Much of the city lay in smouldering rubble and at least 125,000 Berliners had lost their lives. In July 1945, the leaders of the Allies met in Potsdam to carve up Germany and Berlin into four zones of occupation controlled by Britain, the USA, the USSR and France.

Neue Wache

MEMORIAL

5 ⊙ MAP P46, H3

This temple-like neoclassical structure (1818) was Karl Friedrich Schinkel's first important Berlin commission. Originally a royal guardhouse and a memorial to the victims of the Napoleonic Wars, it is now Germany's central memorial for the victims of war and dictatorship. Its sombre and austere interior is dominated by Käthe Kollwitz' heart-wrenching *Pietà*-style sculpture of a mother cradling her dead soldier son. (New Guardhouse; Unter den Linden 4; admission free; ⊙10am-6pm; 🚌100, 245, 300)

Site of Hitler's Bunker

HISTORIC SITE

6 ⊙ MAP P46, D4

Berlin was burning and Soviet tanks advancing when Adolf Hitler shot himself in the head on 30 April 1945 in his bunker near the Reich chancellery. His long-time female companion, Eva Braun, whom he had married just hours earlier, died by his side from a cyanide pill. Today, a parking lot covers the site, revealing its dark history only via an information panel with a diagram of the vast bunker network, construction data and the site's post-WWII history. (cnr In den Ministergärten & Gertrud-Kolmar-Strasse; ⊙24hr; Ⓢ Brandenburger Tor, Ⓤ Brandenburger Tor)

Futurium

MUSEUM

7 ⊙ MAP P46, C1

The future is now at the Futurium, an exhibition space that landed in a suitably spaceship-like structure on the Spree River in late 2019. Divided into three 'thinking spaces' called Nature, People and Technology, it seeks to inspire all of us to participate in the debate on how we are going to – and, more importantly, how we want to – live in the coming decades. (House of Futures; 🕿030-408 189 777; www.futurium. de; Alexanderufer 2; admission free; ⊙10am-6pm Wed & Fri-Mon, to 8pm Thu; 🚻; 🚋M5, M8, M10, Ⓢ Hauptbahnhof, Ⓤ Hauptbahnhof)

Eating

Liu Nudelhaus

CHINESE €

8 🍴 MAP P46, F5

Liu does a roaring trade in food from the southwestern Chinese province of Sichuan, famous for its pandas and its palate-numbing dishes. Must-try: the Sichuan Zajiang noodles bathing in a bold chilli-oil sauce. Come before 12.30pm or after 2pm to avoid the lunchtime rush. (🕿0178 668 4572; https://chengduweidao.de; Kronenstrasse 72; mains €9.50-11.50; ⊙11.30am-3pm Sun-Thu, 11.30am-3pm & 5-8.30pm Fri & Sat; Ⓤ Stadtmitte, Mohrenstrasse)

India Club

NORTH INDIAN €€

9 🍴 MAP P46, D4

No need to book a flight to Mumbai or London: authentic northern Indian cuisine has finally landed in Berlin. Thanks to top toque Manish Bahukhandi, curries here are like culinary poetry, the 24-hour marinated tandoori chicken silky and succulent, and the stuffed cauliflower an inspiration. (☎030-2062 8610; www.india-club-berlin.com; Behrenstrasse 72; mains €18-27; ⏱6-11pm; 🖋; Ⓢ Brandenburger Tor)

Augustiner am Gendarmenmarkt GERMAN €€

10 ⊗ MAP P46, G4

Tourists, concertgoers and hearty-food lovers rub shoulders at rustic tables in this Bavarian-style beer hall. Sausages, roast pork and pretzels provide rib-sticking sustenance, with only a token salad offered for non-carnivores. Service can be uneven. (☎030-2045 4020; www.augustiner-braeu-berlin.de; Charlottenstrasse 55; mains €7.50-30, lunch special €6.40; ⏱10am-10pm; Ⓤ Französische Strasse)

Berliner Republik GASTROPUB €€

11 ⊗ MAP P46, E2

Just as in a mini stock exchange, the price of beer (18 varieties on tap!) fluctuates with demand after 5pm at this tourist-geared riverside pub. Everyone goes Pavlovian when a heavy brass bell rings, signalling rock-bottom prices. A full menu of home-style Berlin and German fare provides sustenance. In summer, seats on the terrace are the most coveted. (☎030-3087 2293; www.die-berliner-republik.de; Schiffbauerdamm 8; mains €10-23; ⏱10am-5am; 🛜; Ⓢ Friedrichstrasse, Ⓤ Friedrichstrasse)

Cookies Cream VEGETARIAN €€€

12 ⊗ MAP P46, F3

In 2017 this perennial local favourite became Berlin's first flesh-free

Neue Wache

MAGMAC83/SHUTTERSTOCK ©

Rebuilt Glamour Pad: Hotel Adlon

On Pariser Platz, overlooking the Brandenburg Gate, the Hotel Adlon is one of Berlin's poshest and most storied hotels. In 1932 the movie *Grand Hotel* starring Greta Garbo was partly filmed here. Destroyed in WWII and rebuilt in the 1990s, today's edition is a near-replica of the 1907 original and remains a favourite haunt of celebs, politicians and the merely moneyed. Remember Michael Jackson dangling his baby out of the window? It happened at the Adlon.

restaurant to enter the Michelin pantheon, on its 10th anniversary no less. Its industrial look and clandestine location are as unorthodox as the tasty compositions of head chef Stephan Hentschel. The entrance is off the service alley of the Westin Grand Hotel (past the chandelier; ring the bell). (📞030-680 730 448; www.cookiescream.com; Behrenstrasse 55; 5-course menu €79, additional courses €10; ⏱5-11pm Tue-Sat; 🍽; Ⓤ Französische Strasse)

Borchardt

INTERNATIONAL €€€

13 🍴 MAP P46, F4

Mick Jagger, George Clooney and Robert Redford are among the celebs who have tucked into dry-aged steaks and plump oysters in the marble-pillared dining hall of this see-and-be-seen Berlin institution,

established in 1853 by a caterer to the Kaiser. No dish, however, moves as fast as the Wiener schnitzel, a wafer-thin slice of breaded veal fried to crisp perfection. (📞030-8188 6262; www.borchardt-restaurant.de; Französische Strasse 47; dinner mains €20-40; ⏱11.30am-midnight; Ⓤ Französische Strasse)

Dachgartenrestaurant Käfer

GERMAN €€€

14 🍴 MAP P46, C2

While politicians debate treaties and taxes in the plenary hall below, you can enjoy breakfast and dinner tasting menus with a regional bent at the restaurant on the Reichstag rooftop. For security reasons, reservations must be made at least two days in advance; they include access to the landmark Reichstag dome. Original picture ID required for entry. (📞030-226 2999; www.feinkost-kaefer.de/berlin; Platz der Republik, enter via West Portal/West C; breakfast from €20.50, 3-course dinner €69, additional courses €10; ⏱9am-1pm & 7-11pm; 🚌100, Ⓤ Bundestag, Ⓢ Brandenburger Tor)

Drinking

Rooftop Terrace

BAR

15 🍷 MAP P46, G3

A hushed, refined ambience reigns at the rooftop bar of the exclusive **Hotel de Rome** (d from €265; Ⓟ➰❄@📶🐾🐾), where you can keep an eye on the Fernsehturm (TV Tower), the opera house and the historic city centre beyond. It's a chill spot for an afternoon coffee break, a sunset cocktail or a romantic glass of champagne under the starry sky. (☎030-460 6090; www.roccofortehotels.com; Behrenstrasse 37, Hotel de Rome; ⏰2-11pm May-Sep; 🛜; 🚌100, 200, TXL, Ⓤ Hausvogteiplatz)

Bar Tausend

BAR

16 🚇 MAP P46, E2

No sign, no light, just an anonymous steel door tucked under a railway bridge leads to one of Berlin's chicest clandestine bars. A mirrored ceiling, a giant light installation resembling an eye and conversation-friendly sounds from soul to house give the tunnel-shaped space a glam, grown-up vibe. Cocktails are inspired by hip districts of the world's metropolises.

(☎030-2758 2070; www.tausendberlin.com; Schiffbauerdamm 11; ⏰7pm-late Thu-Sat; 🚊M1, Ⓢ Friedrichstrasse, Ⓤ Friedrichstrasse)

Entertainment

Staatsoper Berlin

OPERA

17 ⭐ MAP P46, G3

Berlin's most famous opera company performs at the venerable neoclassical Staatsoper Unter den Linden. Its repertory includes works from four centuries along with concerts and classical and modern ballet, all under the musical leadership of Daniel Barenboim. Some performances are shortened to appeal to families. (☎030-2035 4240; www.staatsoper-berlin.de; Unter den Linden 7; tickets €8-180; 👶; 🚌100, 245, 300, Ⓤ Französische Strasse)

Hotel Adlon

FRIMUFILMS/SHUTTERSTOCK ©

Komische Oper OPERA

18 ⭐ MAP P46, F3

The smallest among Berlin's trio of opera houses is also its least stuffy, even if its flashy neo-baroque auditorium might suggest otherwise. Productions are innovative and unconventional – yet top quality – and often reinterpret classic (and sometimes obscure) pieces in zeitgeist-capturing ways. Seats feature an ingenious subtitling system in English, Turkish and other languages. (Comic Opera; 🎫tickets 030-4799 7400; www.komische-oper-berlin.de; Behrenstrasse 55-57; tickets €12-94; 🚌100, 147, 245, 300, Ⓤ Französische Strasse)

Konzerthaus Berlin CLASSICAL MUSIC

19 ⭐ MAP P46, G4

This lovely classical-music venue – a Schinkel design from 1821 –

Free Concerts in Royal Stables

The gifted students at Berlin's top-rated classical music academy, the Hochschule für Musik Hanns Eisler, showcase their talents at up to 400 performances annually, many of them in the **Neuer Marstall** (Schlossplatz 7), where the Prussian royals once kept their coaches and horses. Many concerts are free or low-cost. See the website (www.hfm-berlin.de) for the full schedule.

counts the top-ranked Konzerthausorchester Berlin as its 'house band' but also hosts visiting soloists and orchestras in three halls. For a midday sightseeing break, check the schedule for weekly 45-minute 'Espresso Concerts' costing €8, including one (you guessed it) espresso. (🎫tickets 030-203 092 101; www.konzerthaus.de; Gendarmenmarkt 2; tickets €10-84; Ⓤ Stadtmitte, Französische Strasse)

Pierre Boulez Saal CONCERT VENUE

20 ⭐ MAP P46, H4

Open since 2017, this intimate concert hall was designed by Frank Gehry and conceived by Daniel Barenboim as a venue to promote dialogue between cultures through music. The musical line-up spans the arc from classical to jazz, electronic to Middle Eastern music. (🎫tickets 030-4799 7411; www.boulezsaal.de; Französische Strasse 33d; tickets €10-65; 🚌100, 245, 300, Ⓤ Hausvogteiplatz)

Tipi am Kanzleramt CABARET

21 ⭐ MAP P46, A2

Tipi stages a year-round programme of professional cabaret, dance, acrobatics, musical comedy and magic shows starring German and international acts. It's all presented in a festively decorated cabaret-style tent set up on the edge of Tiergarten park. Pre-show dinner is available. (🎫tickets 030-3906 6550; www.tipi-am-kanzleramt.de; Grosse Querallee; tickets €30-53; 🚌100, Ⓢ Hauptbahnhof, Ⓤ Bundestag)

Shopping

Dussmann – Das Kulturkaufhaus

BOOKS

22 🔒 MAP P46, F3

It's easy to lose track of time in this cultural playground with wall-to-wall books (including an extensive English section), DVDs and CDs, leaving no genre unaccounted for. Bonus points for the downstairs cafe, the vertical garden, and the performance space used for free concerts, political discussions and high-profile book readings and signings. (📞030-2025 1111; www.kulturkaufhaus.de; Friedrichstrasse 90; ⏰9am-10pm Mon-Fri, to 11.30pm Sat; 🛜; ⑤ Friedrichstrasse, Ⓤ Friedrichstrasse)

Ritter Sport Bunte Schokowelt

CHOCOLATE

23 🔒 MAP P46, G4

Fans of Ritter Sport's colourful square chocolate bars can pick up limited-edition, organic, vegan and diet varieties in addition to all the classics at this flagship store. Upstairs, a free exhibit explains the journey from cocoa bean to finished product, but kids are more enchanted by the chocolate kitchen, where staff create your own personalised bars. (📞030-2009 5080; www.ritter-sport.de; Französische Strasse 24; ⏰10am-6pm Mon-Sat; 👶; Ⓤ Französische Strasse)

Rausch Schokoladenhaus

CHOCOLATE

24 🔒 MAP P46, G5

If the Aztecs regarded chocolate as the elixir of the gods, then this emporium of truffles and pralines must be heaven. The shop features Insta-worthy replicas of Berlin landmarks such as Brandenburg Gate, while upstairs you can create your own custom chocolate bar or sip sinful drinking chocolate in the cafe with a view of Gendarmenmarkt. (📞030-757 880; www.rausch.de; Charlottenstrasse 60; ⏰10am-7pm Mon-Sat, from 11am Sun; Ⓤ Stadtmitte)

Galeries Lafayette

DEPARTMENT STORE

25 🔒 MAP P46, F4

Stop by the Berlin branch of the exquisite French fashion emporium, if only to check out the show-stealing interior (designed by Jean Nouvel, no less), centred on a huge glass cone shimmering with kaleidoscopic intensity. Around it wrap three circular floors filled with fancy fashions, fragrances and accessories, while gourmet treats await in the basement food hall. (📞030-209 480; www.galerieslafayette.de; Friedrichstrasse 76-78; ⏰10am-8pm Mon-Sat; Ⓤ Französische Strasse)

Worth a Trip 📷
Experience History at the Jüdisches Museum

In a landmark building by Daniel Libeskind, Berlin's Jewish Museum chronicles Jewish life, history and culture in Germany from the early Middle Ages via the Enlightenment to the community's modern-day renaissance. It's a highly engaging presentation that employs not only original objects but also art installations, interactive games, listening pods and other forms of modern museum curation.

📞 030-2599 3300

www.jmberlin.de

Lindenstrasse 9-14

adult/concession/ under 18yr €8/3/free, audioguide €3

🕙 10am-7pm

Ⓤ Hallesches Tor, Kochstrasse

The Building

Libeskind's architectural masterpiece (which he titled *Between the Lines*) has been interpreted as a 3D metaphor for the tortured history of the Jewish people. Its zigzag shape symbolises a broken Star of David; its silvery titanium-zinc walls are sharply angled; and instead of windows, there are only small gashes piercing the gleaming facade.

The Axes

The museum consists of two buildings. The entrance is via a stately baroque structure that once housed the Prussian supreme court. From here a steep, dark and winding staircase leads down to the Libeskind building and three intersecting walkways (called 'axes') that are a visual allegory for the fates of Jews in the 20th century: death, exile and continuity. Only the latter axis leads to the actual exhibits, but it too is a cumbersome journey up a sloping walkway and several steep flights of stairs.

Permanent Exhibit

Relaunched in August 2020, the museum's new two-floor core exhibit is an engaging trip through 1700 years of history, traditions, trials and triumphs of Jews in Germany. Divided into five historical chapters, it kicks off in the early Middle Ages when Jewish communities first emerged in northwestern Europe. From here, it moves through the Enlightenment and the Nazi years all the way to the present-day revival of Jewish life in Germany. In between, themed areas introduce aspects of Jewish culture and religion, such as music, prayer, the Torah and the Sabbath. Art installations are another highlight, most famously Menashe Kadishman's **Shalekhet – Fallen Leaves**.

★ Top Tips

o Rent the audio-guide for a more in-depth experience.

o Guided tours (in German, €3) take place at 3pm on Saturday and at 11am on Sunday.

o Budget at least two hours to visit the museum, and wear comfortable footwear.

o The garden behind the museum has deckchairs for relaxing and taking in the architecture.

✗ Take a Break

o The museum cafe in the glass courtyard offers light lunches, cakes and hot and cold beverages.

o At the nearby Berlinische Galerie, **Cafe Dix** (☎030-2392 4109; www.cafe-dix. berlin; Alte Jakobstrasse 124-128; mains €6-10; ⏰10am-6pm Wed-Mon; Ⓤ Kochstrasse, Moritzplatz) serves salads, German dishes and cakes.

Explore ✦

Museum Island & Alexanderplatz

Sightseers hit the jackpot in this historic area, headlined by Museum Island, a Unesco-recognised cluster of five world-class repositories brimming with six millennia of artistic expression. The Berliner Dom watches serenely over it all, including the Humboldt Forum cultural centre, which opened in a reconstructed royal palace completed in 2020. For an even grander perspective, ride up the TV Tower, Germany's highest structure.

The Short List

○ **Pergamonmuseum (p60)** *Time-travelling through Ancient Greece and Babylon to the Middle East.*

○ **Neues Museum (p64)** *Making a date with Nefertiti and her royal entourage.*

○ **Humboldt Forum (p69)** *Getting a first look at Berlin's much-anticipated new cultural centre in a reconstructed Prussian city palace.*

○ **DDR Museum (p67)** *Dipping behind the Iron Curtain at this interactive exhibit with its virtual Trabi ride and fully furnished GDR-era apartment.*

Getting There & Around

🚌 100, 245 and 300 travel along Unter den Linden from Alexanderplatz; bus 100 goes to Zoo station via Tiergarten.

Ⓢ S3, S5, S7 and S9 all stop at Hackescher Markt and Alexanderplatz.

Ⓤ U2, U5 and U8 stop at Alexanderplatz. U5 stops at Rotes Rathaus and Museumsinsel. Other handy stations are Klosterstrasse and Märkisches Museum (U2).

Neighbourhood Map on p66

Berliner Dom (p67) CANADASTOCK/SHUTTERSTOCK ©

Top Experience 📷

Discover Treasures at the Pergamonmuseum

Even with the namesake Pergamon Altar off limits for restoration until at least 2023, the Pergamon-museum opens a fascinating window onto the ancient world. Completed in 1930, the palatial three-wing complex presents a feast of classical sculpture and monumental architecture from Greece, Rome, Babylon and the Middle East.

◉ MAP P66, B2

www.smb.museum

adult/concession/under 18yr €12/6/free

🕐 10am-6pm Tue, Wed & Fri-Sun, to 8pm Thu

🚌 100, 245, 300, 🚊 M1, 12, **S** Hackescher Markt, **U** Friedrichstrasse

James-Simon-Galerie

Museumsinsel's central entrance building, the **James-Simon-Galerie** (☎030-266 424 242; www.smb.museum; Bodestrasse) on Bodestrasse, opened in July 2019 and was named for an early-20th-century German-Jewish patron and philanthropist. Designed by David Chipperfield, the colonnaded building contains the ticket office, a cafe and shop, and space for smaller temporary exhibits. It currently provides direct access to the Pergamonmuseum, the Neues Museum and the partly completed Archaeological Promenade, a subterranean walkway that will ultimately link all the island's museums except the Alte Nationalgalerie.

Ishtar Gate

It's impossible not to be awed by the magnificence of the Ishtar Gate (pictured), the **Processional Way** leading to it and the facade of the **king's throne hall**, dating back to Babylon during the reign of King Nebuchadnezzar II (604–562 BCE). All are covered in radiant blue glazed bricks and adorned with ochre reliefs of strutting lions, bulls and dragons representing Babylonian gods. They're so striking, you can almost hear the roaring and fanfare as the procession rolls into town.

Market Gate of Miletus

Merchants and customers once flooded through this splendid 17m-high gate into the bustling market square of Miletus, a wealthy Roman trading town in present-day Turkey. A strong earthquake levelled much of the town in the early Middle Ages, but German archaeologists dug up the site between 1903 and 1905 and managed to put the puzzle back together. The richly decorated marble gate blends Greek and Roman design features and is the world's single largest monument ever to be reassembled in a museum.

★ Top Tips

○ The entrance to the Pergamonmuseum is via the James-Simon-Galerie.

○ Admission is free for those under 18.

○ Arrive early or late on weekdays, and skip the queues by purchasing your ticket online.

○ Make use of the excellent multilanguage audioguides included in the admission price.

✖ Take a Break

○ **Cu29** (www.cu-berlin.de; Eiserne Brücke; dishes €7-15; ⏱noon-6pm Tue, Wed & Fri-Sun, to 8pm Thu) at the James-Simon-Galerie serves elevated cafe fare on the riverside terrace and in the stylish copper-ceilinged interior.

○ Sweet cafe **Petit Bijou** (☎030-3088 2073; www.petitbijou.de; Monbijoustrasse 1; dishes €7-18; ⏱10am-8pm; ☒M1, M5, Ⓢ Oranienburger Strasse) dispenses drinks and snacks – in summer enjoy them from the terrace with a view of the Bode-Museum.

Clay Tablets from Uruk

Founded in the 4th millennium BCE, Uruk (in present-day Iraq) is considered one of the world's first 'mega-cities', with as many as 40,000 inhabitants and more than 9km of city walls. Among the museum's most prized possessions are clay tablets with cuneiform scripts detailing agreements and transactions. They date to the late 4th millennium BCE and are considered among the earliest written documents known to humankind.

Statue of Hadad

A vast room crammed with treasures from ancient Assyria is lorded over by a monumental 2800-year-old statue of a fierce-looking Hadad, the West Semitic god of storm, thunder and rain. Also note the four lion sculptures guarding the partly reconstructed inner gate of the citadel of Samal (in today's Turkey).

Caliph's Palace of Mshatta

When Ottoman Sultan Abdul Hamid II wanted to get into German Emperor Wilhelm II's good graces, he bought him a most generous gift: the facade of the 8th-century palace of Mshatta, in today's Jordan. A masterpiece of early Islamic art, it depicts animals and mythical creatures frolicking peacefully amid a riot of floral motifs in an allusion to the Garden of Eden.

Aleppo Room

Guests arriving at this richly painted, wood-panelled reception room

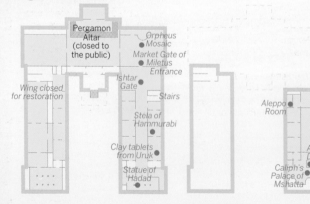

Pergamonmuseum

Pergamon Altar (closed to the public)

Orpheus Mosaic

Market Gate of Miletus Entrance

Wing closed for restoration

Ishtar Gate

Stairs

Stela of Hammurabi

Clay tablets from Uruk

Statue of Hadad

Aleppo Room

Stairs

Alhambra Domed Room

Caliph's Palace of Mshatta

Ground Floor

Upper Floor

would have had no doubt as to the wealth and power of its owner, a Christian merchant in 17th-century Aleppo, Syria. The beautiful, if dizzying, paintings depict both Christian themes and courtly scenes like those portrayed in Persian book illustrations, suggesting a high level of religious tolerance. Look closely to make out the Last Supper to the right of the central door.

Alhambra Domed Roof

A domed cedar and poplar ceiling from the Torre de las Damas (Ladies' Tower) of the Alhambra in southern Spain's Granada forms the 'lid of the Moorish Cabinet' upstairs. Intricately patterned, it centres on a 16-pointed star from which radiate 16 triangular panels inlaid with decorative elements.

Asisi Panorama

While the Pergamon Altar is off limits, you can still grasp its impressive beauty at the exhibit called **Pergamonmuseum. Das Panorama** (☎030-266 424 242; www.smb.museum; Am Kupfergraben 2; adult/concession/under 18yr €12/6/free, combination ticket with Pergamonmuseum €19/9.50/free; ◷10am-6pm Tue-Sun; ▣M1, 12, Ⓤ Friedrichstrasse,

Museum Island Masterplan

The Pergamonmuseum is part of Museum Island (Museumsinsel), a cluster of five museums built between 1830 and 1930 and declared a Unesco World Heritage site in 1999. The distinction was at least partly achieved because of a master plan for the renovation and modernisation of the complex, which is expected to be completed in 2026 under the aegis of British architect David Chipperfield. Except for the Pergamon, now under partial renovation, the restoration of the buildings has been completed. For full details see www.museumsinsel-berlin.de.

Ⓢ Friedrichstrasse, Hackescher Markt) in a purpose-built rotunda opposite the Bode-Museum. Inside is a 360-degree panorama by Iranian artist and architect Yadegar Asisi that presents a vivid photorealistic snapshot of the city of Pergamon in 129 CE under the rule of Roman emperor Hadrian. Also on display are 80 Pergamon masterpieces from the Collection of Antiquities, including a colossal head of Heracles and a big piece from the famous Telephos frieze.

Top Experience 📷

Catch an Exhibit at the Neues Museum

David Chipperfield's reconstruction of the bombed-out Neues Museum (New Museum) on Museum Island is the residence of Queen Nefertiti, the showstopper of the Ägyptisches Museum (Egyptian Museum), alongside the equally enthralling Museum für Vor- und Frühgeschichte (Museum of Pre- and Early History). The British architect incorporated every original shard, scrap and brick he could find into the new building, creating a dynamic blend of the historic and the modern.

◎ MAP P66, B3

www.smb.museum

adult/concession/under 18yr €12/6/free

🕙10am-6pm Tue, Wed & Fri-Sun, to 8pm Thu

🚌100, 245, 300, 🚊M1, 12, Ⓢ Hackescher Markt, Ⓤ Friedrichstrasse

Nefertiti

An audience with Berlin's most beautiful woman, the 3300-year-old Egyptian Queen Nefertiti (pictured) – she of the long graceful neck and eternally good looks – is a must. Extremely well preserved, the sculpture was part of the treasure trove unearthed around 1912 by a Berlin expedition of archaeologists who were sifting through the sands of Armana, the royal city built by Nefertiti's husband, King Akhenaten.

Berliner Goldhut

Resembling a wizard's hat, the 3000-year-old Berlin Gold Hat must indeed have struck the Bronze Age people as something magical. The entire cone is swathed in elaborate bands of astrological symbols believed to have helped priests calculate the movements of sun and moon, and thus predict the best times for planting and harvesting. It's one of only four unearthed worldwide.

Berlin Grüner Kopf

Another famous work is the so-called Berlin Green Head – the bald head of a priest carved from smooth green stone. Created around 400 BCE in the Late Egyptian Period, it shows Greek influence and is unusual in that it is not an actual portrait of a specific person but an idealised figure meant to exude universal wisdom and experience.

Trojan Collection

In 1870 German archaeologist Heinrich Schliemann discovered a stunning hoard of treasures from ancient Troy while digging around near Hisarlik in modern-day Turkey. Alas, most of the elaborate jewellery, ornate weapons and gold mugs on display are replicas because the originals became Soviet war booty after WWII and remain in Moscow.

★ Top Tips

○ Skip the queue by buying advance tickets online.

○ If you plan on visiting more than one museum, save money by buying the combination ticket (€19, concession €9.50), good for one-day admission to all five museums and the Asisi Panorama.

○ Admission is free for those under 18.

○ The entrance is via the James-Simon-Galerie.

✕ Take a Break

○ A 250m walk away, the **Allegretto Gran Cafe** (☎030-308 777 517; http://allegretto-grancaffe.de; Anna-Louisa-Karsch-Strasse 2; mains €10-20; ⏱noon-9pm Mon-Fri, 10am-9pm Sat & Sun; 🛜; 🚌100, 200, 245, Ⓢ Hackescher Markt) serves coffee and cake, a light lunch and traditional German mains with views of the Spree and the Berliner Dom.

Museum Island & Alexanderplatz

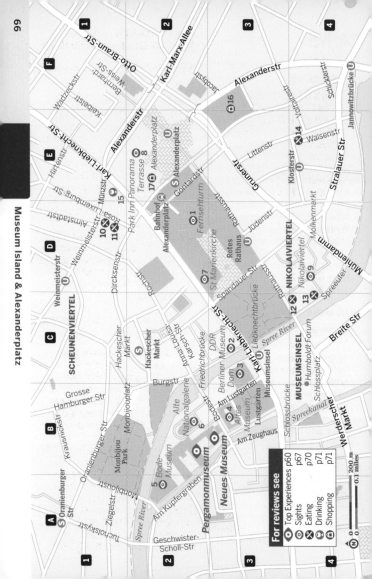

Grosse Hamburger Str

Oranienburger Str

SCHEUNENVIERTEL

Hackescher Markt

MUSEUMSINSEL

Humboldt Forum

NIKOLAIVIERTEL

Alexanderplatz

Park Inn Panorama Terrasse 8

Fernsehturm

St Marienkirche

Rotes Rathaus

Pergamonmuseum

Neues Museum

Bode Museum

Altes Museum

Berliner Museum

DDR Museum

Monbijou Park

Monbijouplatz

Spree River

Karl-Marx-Allee

Otto-Braun-Str

Bernhard-Weiss-Str

Karl-Liebknecht-Str

Rosa-Luxemburg-Str

Münzstr

Almstadtstr

Weinmeisterstr

Dircksenstr

Rochstr

Spandauer Str

Rathausstr

Grunerstr

Littenstr

Klosterstr

Waisenstr

Stralauer Str

Mühlendamm

Molkenmarkt

Spreeufer

Breite Str

Werderscher Markt

Spreekanal

Schlossbrücke

Am Lustgarten

Lustgarten

Am Zeughaus

Bodestr

Am Kupfergraben

Friedrichbrücke

Anna-Louisa-Karsch-Str

Burgstr

Karl-Liebknecht-Str

Jüdenstr

Gontardstr

Alexanderstr

Jacobystr

Alexanderstr

Schicklerstr

Voltairestr

Jannowitzbrücke

200 m
0.1 miles

Sights

Fernsehturm
LANDMARK

1 ◉ MAP P66, D2

Germany's tallest structure, the TV Tower has been soaring 368m high since 1969 and is as iconic to Berlin as the Eiffel Tower is to Paris. On clear days, views are stunning from the observation deck (with bar) at 203m or from the upstairs (207m) **Sphere restaurant** (mains €10-33; ⏱10am-10pm; 📶), which makes one revolution per hour. (TV Tower; 📞030-247 575 875; www.tv-turm. de; Panoramastrasse 1a; adult/child €18.50/9.50, fast track online ticket €22.50/13; ⏱9am-midnight Mar-Oct, 10am-midnight Nov-Feb, last ascent 11.30pm; 🚌100, 200, 300, Ⓤ Alexanderplatz, Ⓢ Alexanderplatz)

DDR Museum
MUSEUM

2 ◉ MAP P66, C3

This touchy-feely museum does an insightful and entertaining job of pulling back the Iron Curtain on daily life in socialist East Germany. You'll learn how kids were put through collective potty training, engineers earned little more than farmers, and everyone, it seems, went on nudist holidays. A perennial crowd-pleaser among the historic objects on display is a Trabi, the tinny East German standard car – sit in it and take a virtual spin around an East Berlin neighbourhood. (GDR (East Germany) Museum; 📞030-847 123 731; www.ddr-museum. de; Karl-Liebknecht-Strasse 1; adult/

concession €9.80/6; ⏱9am-9pm; 🚌100, 247, 300, Ⓢ Hackescher Markt)

Berliner Dom
CATHEDRAL

3 ◉ MAP P66, C3

Pompous yet majestic, the Italian Renaissance–style former royal court church (1905) does triple duty as house of worship, museum and concert hall. Inside it's gilt to the hilt and outfitted with a lavish marble-and-onyx altar, a 7269-pipe Sauer organ and elaborate royal sarcophagi. Climb up the 267 steps to the gallery for glorious city views. (Berlin Cathedral; 📞ticket office 030-2026 9136; www.berlinerdom.de; Am Lustgarten; adult/concession/under 18yr €7/5/free; ⏱hours vary, usually 9am-8pm Apr-Sep, to 7pm Oct-Mar; 🚌100, 247, 300, Ⓢ Hackescher Markt, Ⓤ Rotes Rathaus)

Altes Museum
MUSEUM

4 ◉ MAP P66, B3

A curtain of fluted columns gives way to the Pantheon–inspired rotunda of the grand neoclassical Old Museum, which harbours a prized antiquities collection. In the downstairs galleries, sculptures, vases, tomb reliefs and jewellery shed light on various facets of life in ancient Greece, while upstairs the focus is on the Etruscans and Romans. Top draws include the *Praying Boy* bronze sculpture, Roman silver vessels, an 'erotic cabinet' (over 18s only!), and portraits of Caesar and Cleopatra. (📞030-266 424 242; www.smb.museum; Am Lustgarten; adult/concession/under 18yr €10/5/

free; ⏰10am-6pm Tue, Wed & Fri-Sun, to 8pm Thu; 🚌100, 245, 300, 🚊M1, 12, Ⓢ Friedrichstrasse, Hackescher Markt, Ⓤ Friedrichstrasse)

Bode-Museum MUSEUM

5 ◎ MAP P66, A2

On the northern tip of Museumsinsel, this palatial edifice houses a comprehensive collection of European sculpture from the early Middle Ages to the 18th century, including priceless masterpieces by Tilman Riemenschneider, Antonio Canova and Giovanni Pisano. Other rooms harbour a precious coin collection and a smattering of Byzantine art, including sarcophagi and ivory carvings. (📞030-266 424 242; www.smb.museum; cnr Am Kupfergraben & Monbijoubrücke; adult/concession/under 18yr €10/5/free; ⏰10am-6pm Tue, Wed & Fri-Sun, to 8pm Thu; 🚌100, 245, 300, 🚊M1, 12, Ⓢ Hackescher Markt, Friedrichstrasse, Ⓤ Friedrichstrasse)

Alte Nationalgalerie MUSEUM

6 ◎ MAP P66, B2

The Greek temple–style Old National Gallery is a three-storey showcase of 19th-century European art. To get a sense of the period's virtuosity, pay special attention to the moody landscapes by romantic heart-throb Caspar David Friedrich, the epic canvases by Franz Krüger and Adolf Menzel glorifying Prussia, the Gothic fantasies of Karl Friedrich Schinkel, and the sprinkling of works by French and German impressionists. (📞030-266 424 242;

www.smb.museum; Bodestrasse 1-3; adult/concession/under 18yr €10/5/free; ⏰10am-6pm Tue, Wed & Fri-Sun, to 8pm Thu; 🚌100, 245, 300, Ⓢ Hackescher Markt, Alexanderplatz)

St Marienkirche CHURCH

7 ◎ MAP P66, D2

This Gothic brick gem has welcomed worshippers since the early 14th century, making it one of Berlin's oldest surviving churches. A 22m-long *Dance of Death* fresco in the vestibule inspired by a 15th-century plague leads to a relatively plain interior enlivened by numerous other art treasures. The oldest is the 1437 bronze baptismal font buttressed by a trio of dragons. The baroque alabaster pulpit by Andreas Schlüter from 1703 is another eye-catcher. (St Mary's Church; www.marienkirche-berlin.de; Karl-Liebknecht-Strasse 8; ⏰10am-6pm Apr-Dec, to 4pm Jan-Mar; 🚌100, 200, 245, 300, Ⓢ Hackescher Markt, Alexanderplatz, Ⓤ Alexanderplatz, Rotes Rathaus)

Park Inn Panorama Terrasse VIEWPOINT

8 ◎ MAP P66, E2

For sweeping city views at eye level with the Fernsehturm (TV Tower), head up to the rooftop Panorama Terrasse, the open-air lounge of the Park Inn hotel, some 120m above Alexanderplatz. Grab a sunlounger and relax with a cold beer or a glass of bubbly. There's a lift, of course, but it's stairs for the last five floors. (📞030-238 90;

Humboldt Forum: Berlin's New Cultural Quarter

After seven years in the making, the **Humboldt Forum** (Map p66, C4; 030-265 9500; www.humboldtforum.org; Schlossplatz; admission free; 100, 247, 300, Rotes Rathaus), Berlin's new culture and science hub inside a replica of the baroque Prussian city palace, was completed in December 2020 and opened in mid-2021. Conceived to create a dynamic dialogue between the arts and sciences, it will ultimately house museums, exhibits, an interactive science lab and other spaces, accompanied by a lively program of performances, films and lectures that explore topical issues in science, art, religion, politics and business. Admission is free but you need a timed ticket to enter (available online).

Exhibits focus on the **800-year history** of the site, including vestiges of the original palace, and on the complex' namesakes, the Enlightenment thinkers and brothers **Alexander and Wilhelm Humboldt**. At the **Humboldt Lab** you can engage with the sciences to gain a better understanding of this increasingly complex world, while **Berlin Global** examines the city of Berlin and its connections with the world through such themes as revolution and entertainment. A highlight will be the opening of the **Ethnological Museum** and the **Asian Art Museum**.

Although barely damaged in WWII, the grand palace where Prussian rulers had made their home since 1443 was blown up by East Germany's government in 1950 to drop the final curtain on Prussian and Nazi rule. To emphasise the point, the new communist rulers built their own modernist parliament – called Palast der Republik (Palace of the Republic) – on top of the ruins 26 years later. Riddled with asbestos, it too had a date with the wrecking ball in 2006.

www.parkinn-berlin.de/en/panorama-terrace; Alexanderplatz 7; €4; noon-10pm Apr-Sep, to 6pm Oct-Mar; Alexanderplatz, Alexanderplatz)

Nikolaiviertel AREA

9 MAP P66, D4

Commissioned by the East German government to celebrate Berlin's 750th birthday, the twee Nicholas Quarter is a half-hearted attempt at recreating the city's medieval birthplace around its oldest surviving building, the 1230 Nikolaikirche. The maze of cobbled lanes is worth a quick stroll, while several olde-worlde-style restaurants provide sustenance. (btwn Rathausstrasse, Breite Strasse, Spandauer Strasse & Mühlendamm; admission free; 24hr; Klosterstrasse)

Eating

Dolores
CALIFORNIAN €

10 🗷 MAP P66, D1

Dolores hasn't put a foot wrong since introducing the California–style burrito to Berlin. Pick your favourites from among the marinated meats (or soy meat), rice, beans, veggies, cheeses and homemade salsas, and the cheerful staff will build it on the spot. Goes perfectly with an *agua fresca* (Mexican–style lemonade). (📞030-2809 9597; www.dolores-online.de; Rosa-Luxemburg-Strasse 7; burritos from €5.50; ⏰11.30am-9pm; 🛜🍽; ⓤAlexanderplatz, Ⓢ Alexanderplatz)

Good Bank
HEALTH FOOD €

11 🗷 MAP P66, D1

Good Bank made headlines as the country's first 'vertical-farm-to-table restaurant' for growing lettuces right in its tunnel-shaped space. The freshly harvested leaves find their destiny in an array of eclectic salads and colourful organic rice- or quinoa-based bowls. A great lunch option. (📞030-3302 1410; www.good-bank.de; Rosa-Luxemburg-Strasse 5; mains €6-10; ⏰11.30am-10pm; 🍽; ⓤAlexanderplatz, Ⓢ Alexanderplatz)

Ngon
VIETNAMESE €€

12 🗷 MAP P66, C4

Ngon is Berlin's first authentic Vietnamese restaurant to spotlight all layers of the country's culinary tradition, from mild in the north to spicy in the middle and fruity-sweet in the south. Move from creatively filled rolls to rich beef *pho* and the unmissable 'Tofu is on Fire' (a veg-seafood-tofu medley), all gorgeously presented in a sensuously lit setting with private-villa flair. (📞0174 192 3359; www.ngonberlin.com; Rathausstrasse 23; mains €12-22; ⏰5pm-midnight Mon-Thu, noon-midnight Fri-Sun; ⓤAlexanderplatz, Rotes Rathaus)

Brauhaus Georgbraeu
GERMAN €€

13 🗷 MAP P66, C4

Solidly on the tourist track, this old-style gastropub churns out its own light and dark Georg-Braeu beer, which can even be ordered by the metre (12 glasses at 0.2L). In winter the woodsy beer hall is perfect for tucking into hearty Berlin–style fare, while in summer tables in the riverside beer garden are golden. (📞030-242 4244; www.brauhaus-georgbraeu.de; Spreeufer 4; mains €7-16; ⏰noon-midnight; ⓤAlexanderplatz, Rotes Rathaus)

Zur Letzten Instanz
GERMAN €€

14 🗷 MAP P66, E4

With its folksy Old Berlin charm, this rustic restaurant has been an enduring hit since 1621 and has fed everyone from Napoleon and Charlie Chaplin to Angela Merkel. Although geared to tourists, it serves quality regional rib-stickers such as grilled pork knuckle or meatballs in caper sauce. In summer the beer garden beckons.

(☎ 030-242 5528; www.zurletzten instanz.com; Waisenstrasse 14-16; mains €14-26; ⏱ noon-midnight Tue-Sun; Ⓤ Klosterstrasse)

Drinking

Braufactum Berlin   CRAFT BEER

15 Ⓡ MAP P66, E1

With its urban-contempo looks and big terrace, this craft-beer outpost shakes up the gastro wasteland of Alexanderplatz. Aside from the dozen house brews like the subtly sweet-bitter India Pale Ale Progusta and the whisky-barrel-matured Barrel 1, the blackboard menu also features suds from other breweries. Solid pub grub (€7 to €10) helps keep brains in balance. (☎ 030-8471 2959; www.braufactum-alexanderplatz. de; Memhardstrasse 1; ⏱ noon-late; Ⓤ Alexanderplatz, Ⓢ Alexanderplatz)

Shopping

Alexa   MALL

16 Ⓐ MAP P66, F3

Power shoppers love this XXL mall, which cuts a rose-hued presence near Alexanderplatz and features the predictable range of high-street retailers. Good food court for a bite on the run. (www. alexacentre.com; Grunerstrasse 20; ⏱ 10am-9pm Mon-Sat; Ⓢ Alexander-platz, Ⓤ Alexanderplatz)

Galeria Kaufhof   DEPARTMENT STORE

17 Ⓐ MAP P66, E2

A full makeover by Josef Paul Klei-hues turned this former GDR–era department store into a glitzy retail cube, complete with a glass-domed light court and a sleek travertine skin that glows green at night. There's little you won't find on the five football-field-size floors, includ-ing a gourmet supermarket on the ground floor. (☎ 030-247 430; www. galeria.de; Alexanderplatz 9; ⏱ 10am-8pm Mon-Wed, to 9pm Thu-Sat; Ⓢ Alex-anderplatz, Ⓤ Alexanderplatz)

Explore

Potsdamer Platz

This new quarter, forged from ground once bisected by the Berlin Wall, is a showcase of contemporary architecture and home to museums, a multiplex cinema and hotels. Culture lovers should not skip the nearby Kulturforum museums, especially the Gemäldegalerie, which sits right next to the world-class Berliner Philharmonie and the leafy Tiergarten park.

The Short List

○ **Gemäldegalerie (p74)** *Perusing an Aladdin's cave of old masters – from Rembrandt to Vermeer.*

○ **Sony Center (p79)** *Standing beneath the magnificent canopy of this svelte glass-and-steel landmark.*

○ **Panoramapunkt (p79)** *Catching Europe's fastest lift to take in Berlin's impressive cityscape.*

○ **Tiergarten (p80)** *Getting lost amid the lawns, trees and leafy paths of this sprawling city park.*

Getting There & Around

🚌 Line 200 links with Zoologischer Garten and Alexanderplatz; 300 with the East Side Gallery; M41 with Hauptbahnhof, Kreuzberg and Neukölln; and M29 with Kreuzberg and Charlottenburg via Checkpoint Charlie.

Ⓢ S1 and S2 link Potsdamer Platz with Unter den Linden and the Scheunenviertel.

Ⓤ U2 stops at Potsdamer Platz and Mendelssohn-Bartholdy-Park.

Neighbourhood Map on p84

Tiergarten (p80) SVETLANA TURCHENICK/SHUTTERSTOCK ©

Top Experience 📷
Admire Art at the Gemäldegalerie

The Gemäldegalerie (Gallery of Old Masters) ranks among the world's finest and most comprehensive collections of European art from the 13th to the 18th centuries. Expect to feast your eyes on masterpieces by Titian, Goya, Botticelli, Holbein, Gainsborough, Canaletto, Hals, Rubens, Vermeer and many other old masters. The gallery also hosts high-profile visiting exhibits featuring works by the great artists of this period.

◉ **MAP P84, A2**

www.smb.museum/gg

adult/concession/under 18yr €10/5/free

🕙 10am-6pm Tue, Wed & Fri, to 8pm Thu, 11am-6pm Sat & Sun

🚌 200, 300, M41, M48, M85, **S** Potsdamer Platz, **U** Potsdamer Platz

Hieronymus Holzschuher (1526)

Room 2

Hieronymus Holzschuher was a Nuremberg patrician, a career politician and a strong supporter of the Reformation. He was also a friend of one of the greatest German Renaissance painters, Albrecht Dürer. In this portrait, which shows its sitter at age 57, the artist brilliantly lasers in on Holzschuher's features with utmost precision, down to the furrows, wrinkles and thinning hair.

Portrait of a Young Woman (1470)

Room 4

Berlin's own *Mona Lisa* may not be as famous as the real thing but she's quite intriguing nonetheless. Who is this woman with the almond-shaped eyes and porcelain skin who gazes straight at us with a blend of sadness and scepticism? This famous portrait is a key work by Petrus Christus and his only one depicting a woman.

Fountain of Youth (1546)

Room III

Lucas Cranach the Elder's poignant painting illustrates humankind's yearning for eternal youth. Old crones plunge into a pool of water and emerge as dashing hotties – this fountain would surely put plastic surgeons out of business. The transition is reflected in the landscape, which is stark and craggy on the left, and lush and fertile on the right.

Dutch Proverbs (1559)

Room 7

In this moralistic yet humorous painting, Dutch Renaissance painter Pieter Bruegel the Elder manages to illustrate more than 100 proverbs and idioms in a single seaside village scene. While some emphasise the absurdity of human behaviour, others unmask its imprudence and sinfulness. Some sayings are still in use today, among them 'swimming against the tide' and 'armed to the teeth'.

★ **Top Tips**

○ Take advantage of the excellent free audioguide to get the low-down on selected works.

○ Note that the room numbering system is quite confusing as both Latin (I, II, III) and Arabic numbers (1, 2, 3) are used.

○ Paintings are occasionally rehung, so room numbers listed here are subject to change.

○ A tour of all 72 rooms covers almost 2km, so allow at least a couple of hours for your visit and wear comfortable shoes.

✖ **Take a Break**

○ The friendly **Chez Ahmet** kiosk on Potsdamer Strasse has cold drinks, *Currywurst* and Turkish snacks from 10am to 8pm.

Potsdamer Platz Admire Art at the Gemäldegalerie

Malle Babbe (1633)

Room 13

Frans Hals ingeniously captures the character and vitality of his subject, 'Crazy Barbara', with free-wielding brushstrokes. Hals met the woman with the almost demonic laugh in the workhouse for the mentally ill where his son Pieter was also a resident. The tin mug and owl are symbols of Babbe's fondness for tipple.

Mennonite Minister Cornelius Claesz Anslo (1641)

Room X

A masterpiece in the gallery's prized Rembrandt collection, this large-scale canvas shows the cloth merchant and Mennonite preacher Anslo in conversation with his wife.

The huge open Bible and his gesturing hand sticking out in almost 3D style from the centre of the painting are meant to emphasise the strength of his religious convictions.

Woman with a Pearl Necklace (1662–64)

Room 18

No, it's not the *Girl with a Pearl Earring* of book and movie fame, but it's still one of Jan Vermeer's most famous paintings: a young woman studies herself in the mirror while fastening a pearl necklace. A top dog among Dutch realist painters, Vermeer mesmerises viewers by beautifully capturing this intimate moment with characteristic soft brushstrokes.

Gemäldegalerie

Portrait of John Wilkinson (1775)

Room 20

Works by Thomas Gainsborough are rarely seen outside the UK, which is what makes this portrait of British industrialist John Wilkinson so special. Nicknamed 'Iron Mad Wilkinson' for pioneering the making and use of cast iron, here he is – somewhat ironically – shown in a natural setting, almost blending in with his surroundings.

Il Campo di Rialto (1758–63)

Room XII

Giovanni Antonio Canal, aka Canaletto, studied painting in the workshop of his theatre-set-designer father. Here he depicts the Campo di Rialto, the arcaded main market square of his hometown, Venice, with stunning precision and perspective. Note the goldsmith shops on the left, the wig-wearing merchants in the centre and the stores selling paintings and furniture on the right.

Amor Victorious (1602–03)

Room XIV

That's quite a cheeky fellow peering down on viewers, isn't it? Wearing nothing but a mischievous grin and a pair of black angel wings, with a fistful of arrows, this Amor means business. In this famous painting, Caravaggio shows off his amazing talent at depicting objects with near-photographic realism achieved by his ingeniously theatrical use of light and shadow.

Leda & the Swan (1532)

Room XV

Judging by her blissed-out expression, Leda is having a fine time with that swan who, according to Greek mythology, is none other than Zeus himself. The erotically charged nature of this painting by Italian Renaissance artist Correggio apparently so incensed its one-time owner Louis of Orléans that he cut off Leda's head with a knife. It was later restored.

Madonna with Child & Singing Angels (1477)

Room XVIII

Renaissance artist Sandro Botticelli's circular painting (a format called a tondo) is a symmetrical composition showing Mary at the centre flanked by two sets of four wingless angels. It's an intimate moment that shows the Virgin tenderly embracing – perhaps even about to breastfeed – her child. The white lilies are symbols of her purity.

Top Experience 📷
Wander Around Potsdamer Platz

The rebirth of the historic Potsdamer Platz was Europe's biggest building project of the 1990s, a showcase of urban renewal masterminded by such top international architects as Renzo Piano and Helmut Jahn. An entire city quarter sprouted on terrain once bifurcated by the Berlin Wall and today houses offices, theatres and cinemas, hotels, apartments and museums.

◉ MAP P84, C2

Alte Potsdamer Strasse

🚍 200, 300, M41,
Ⓢ Potsdamer Platz,
Ⓤ Potsdamer Platz

Sony Center

Designed by Helmut Jahn, the visually dramatic **Sony Center** (www.potsdamer-platz.net) is fronted by a 26-floor, glass-and-steel tower that integrates architectural relics from the pre-war Potsdamer Platz. A tentlike glass roof with supporting beams radiating like bicycle spokes canopies a central cafe-ringed plaza.

Museum für Film und Fernsehen

From silent movies to sci-fi, Germany's long and illustrious film history gets the star treatment at the **Museum für Film und Fernsehen** (030-300 9030; www.deutsche-kinemathek.de; adult/concession €8/5, 4-8pm Thu free; 10am-6pm Wed & Fri-Mon, to 8pm Thu). Major themes include pioneers and early divas, silent-era classics such as Fritz Lang's *Metropolis,* Leni Riefenstahl's groundbreaking Nazi-era documentary *Olympia,* German exiles in Hollywood and diva extraordinaire Marlene Dietrich.

Panoramapunkt

A speedy lift yo-yos up the red-brick postmodern Kollhoff Tower to the **Panoramapunkt** (030-2593 7080; www.panoramapunkt.de; adult/concession €7.50/6, without wait €11.50/9; 11am-7pm Apr-Oct, to 5pm Nov-Mar) viewing platform in 20 seconds. From 100m you can pinpoint the sights, make a stop in the 1930s-style cafe, enjoy sunset from the terrace and check out the history exhibit.

Daimler Contemporary Berlin

Ring the bell to be buzzed into the free **Daimler Contemporary Berlin** (030-2594 1421; www.art.daimler.com; 11am-6pm), which showcases international abstract, conceptual and minimalist art. It's on the top floor of the 1912 **Haus Huth**, the only Potsdamer Platz structure that survived WWII intact.

★ Top Tips

○ Check out the Berlin Wall segments outside the Potsdamer Platz S-Bahn station entrance.

○ Admission to the Museum für Film und Fernsehen is free from 4pm to 8pm Thursdays.

○ An original Berlin Wall guard tower is just a short walk away on Erna-Berger-Strasse (off Stresemannstrasse).

○ The Boulevard der Stars honours German TV and film celebrities like Marlene Dietrich with brass stars embedded on the median strip of Potsdamer Strasse.

✕ Take a Break

○ Take time out with a single-origin cuppa or a coffee-based cocktail at the Barn (p90), inside the historic Haus Huth.

○ Restore energy with a colourful, health-focused lunch at Ki-Nova (p89), an upbeat cafe with sidewalk tables.

Walking Tour 🥾

A Leisurely Tiergarten Stroll

Berlin's rulers used to hunt boar and pheasants in the rambling Tiergarten until garden architect Peter Lenné landscaped the grounds in the 18th century. Today it's one of the world's largest urban parks, popular for strolling, jogging, picnicking, Frisbee tossing and sunbathing. Walking across the entire park takes at least an hour, but even a shorter stroll has its rewards.

Walk Facts

Start Brandenburg Gate;
U-Bahn Brandenburger Tor,
S-Bahn Brandenburger Tor

End Potsdamer Platz;
U-Bahn Potsdamer Platz,
S-Bahn Potsdamer Platz

Length 4km; two hours

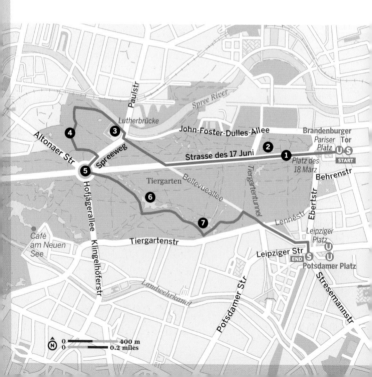

❶ Strasse des 17 Juni

The broad boulevard bisecting Tiergarten was named Street of 17 June in honour of the victims of the bloodily quashed 1953 workers' uprising in East Berlin. Back in the 16th century, the road linked two royal palaces; it was doubled in width and turned into a triumphal road under Hitler.

❷ Sowjetisches Ehrenmal

Berlin lay in ruins when the imposing Soviet War Memorial was dedicated in November 1945. It is one of three in the city that honours the 80,000 Soviet soldiers who died in the Battle of Berlin, including the 2000 buried behind its colonnades. The memorial's entrance is flanked by two Russian T-34 tanks, said to have been the first to enter the city.

❸ Schloss Bellevue

A succession of German presidents have made their home in snowy-white Bellevue Palace on the edge of the Tiergarten. The neoclassical pile was originally a pad for the youngest brother of King Frederick the Great. It became a school under Kaiser Wilhelm II and a museum of ethnology under the Nazis. It's closed to the public.

❹ Teehaus im Englischen Garten

In a hidden corner of Tiergarten, this reed-thatched **teahouse** (📞030-3948 0400; www.teehaus-tiergarten.com; mains €8.50-28.50; ⏰noon-11pm Tue-Sat, from 10am Sun; 🚶) is an idyllic spot, especially in summer when the beer garden gets packed. Free concerts on Sundays in July and August.

❺ Siegessäule

Engulfed by roundabout traffic, the 1873 Victory Column was erected to celebrate Prussian military victories and is now a prominent symbol of Berlin's gay community. The gilded woman on top represents the goddess of victory and is featured prominently in the Wim Wenders movie *Wings of Desire*. The column originally stood in front of the Reichstag until the Nazis moved it here in 1938. Climb to the top to appreciate the park's dimensions.

❻ Rousseauinsel

One of Tiergarten's most idyllic spots is the Rousseauinsel, a teensy island in a placid pond that's a memorial to 18th-century French philosopher Jean-Jacques Rousseau. It was designed to resemble his actual burial site on an island near Paris. Look for the stone pillar.

❼ Luiseninsel

Another enchanting place, Luiseninsel is a tranquil gated garden brimming with statues and resplendent with seasonal flower beds. It was created after Napoleon's occupying troops left town in 1808 in celebration of the return from exile of the royal couple King Friedrich Wilhelm III and Queen Luise.

Walking Tour 🥾

Walking the Wall

Construction of the Berlin Wall began shortly after midnight on 13 August 1961. For the next 28 years this grim barrier divided a city and its people, becoming the most visible symbol of the Cold War. By now the city's halves have visually merged so perfectly that it takes a keen eye to tell East from West. To give you a sense of the period of division, this walk follows the most central section of the Berlin Wall.

Walk Facts

Start Checkpoint Charlie; U-Bahn Kochstrasse/ Checkpoint Charlie

End Parlament der Bäume; U-Bahn Bundestag

Length 3km; two hours

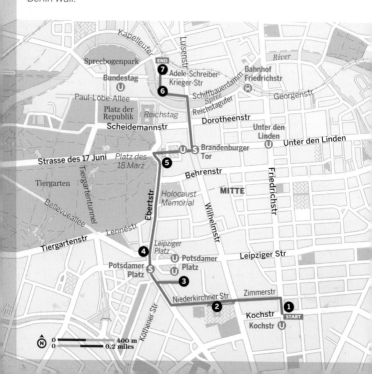

❶ Checkpoint Charlie

As the third Allied checkpoint, Checkpoint Charlie (p85) got its name from the third letter in the NATO phonetic alphabet. Weeks after the Wall was built, US and Soviet tanks faced off here in one of the tensest moments of the Cold War.

❷ Niederkirchner Strasse

Along Niederkirchner Strasse looms a 200m-long section of the original outer border wall. Scarred by souvenir hunters, it's now protected by a fence. The border strip was very narrow here, with the inner wall abutting such buildings as the former Nazi Air Force Ministry on the corner of Niederkirchner Strasse and Wilhelmstrasse.

❸ Border Watchtower

Imagine what it was like to be a Berlin Wall border guard when climbing up the iron ladder of one of the few remaining watchtowers. The octagonal observation perch of this 1969 model was particularly cramped and later replaced by larger square towers.

❹ Potsdamer Platz

Potsdamer Platz used to be a massive no-man's land bisected by the Wall and a 'death strip' several hundred metres wide. Outside the northern S-Bahn station entrance are a few Berlin Wall segments.

❺ Brandenburg Gate

The Brandenburg Gate (p42) was where construction of the Wall began. Many heads of state gave speeches in front of it, including former US president Ronald Reagan who, in 1987, uttered the famous words: 'Mr Gorbachev, tear down this wall!'

❻ Mauer-Mahnmal

In the basement of the **Marie-Elisabeth-Lüders-Haus** (www.bundestag.de; Schiffbauerdamm; admission free; ⊙ galleries 11am-5pm Tue-Sun; Ⓢ Hauptbahnhof, Ⓤ Bundestag, Hauptbahnhof), which houses the parliamentary library, is the Mauer-Mahnmal, an art installation by Ben Wagin that runs along the original course of the Berlin Wall. It consists of original segments, each painted with the number of people killed at the Wall during each of the 28 years it divided the city. Approach from the Spree promenade. If it's closed, you can easily sneak a peak through the glass front of the building.

❼ Parlament der Bäume

Wagin also created the Parliament of Trees, a charmingly unruly garden and art installation. It consists of original Wall slabs and granite plaques engraved with the names of 258 people who died trying to cross the Wall.

A	1	
B	2	
C	3	
D	4	
E		
F		

For reviews see

⊙ Top Experiences	p74
⊙ Sights	p85
⊗ Eating	p88
⊕ Drinking	p90
⊕ Entertainment	p91
⊕ Shopping	p91

TIERGARTEN

Tiergarten

In den Ministergärten

Kemperplatz

Lennéstr

Bellevuestr

Ben-Gurion-Str

Tiergartenstr

Musikinstrumenten-Museum

Kunstgewerbemuseum

Sigismundstr

Gedenkstätte Deutscher Widerstand

Matthäikirchplatz

Gemäldegalerie

Kupferstichkabinett

Kulturforum

Reichpietschufer

Landwehrkanal

Lützowstr

Lützowufer

Potsdamer Str

Pohlstr

Kurfürstenstr

Gleisdreieck

Flottwellstr

Schöneberger Ufer

Tempelhofer Ufer

Hallesches Ufer

Schöneberger Str

Möckernstr

WESTERN KREUZBERG

Anhalter Bahnhof

Berlin Story Bunker

Askanischer Platz

Dessauer Str

Mendelssohn-Bartholdy-Park

Stresemannstr

Anhalter Str

Stresemannstr

Gröpiusbau

Topographie des Terrors

Niederkirchner Str

Wilhelmstr

Leipziger Str

Mohrenstr

Taubenstr

Friedrichstadtpassagen

Stadtmitte

Mauerstr

Leipziger Str

Friedrichstr

Schützenstr

Zimmerstr

Kochstr

Kochstr

Checkpoint Charlie

Rudi-Dutschke-Str

Charlottenstr

Markgrafenstr

Lindenstr

Ritterstr

Berlinische Galerie

Franz-Klühs-Str

KREUZBERG

Vossstr

Potsdamer Platz

Leipziger Platz

Potsdamer Platz

Alte Potsdamer Str

Marlene-Dietrich-Platz

Gabriele-Tergit-Promenade

Linkstr

Kothener Str

Potsdamer Brücke

Potsdamer Platz

N

0 400 m
0 0.2 miles

Sights

Topographie des Terrors

MUSEUM

1  MAP P84, D2

In the spot where the most feared institutions of Nazi Germany (the Gestapo headquarters, the SS central command and the Reich Security Main Office) once stood, this compelling exhibit documents the stages of terror and persecution, puts a face on the perpetrators, and details the impact these brutal institutions had on all of Europe. A second exhibit outside zeroes in on how life changed for Berlin and its people after the Nazis made it their capital. (Topography of Terror; ☎030-2545 0950; www.topographie. de; Niederkirchner Strasse 8; admission free; ☻10am-8pm, grounds close dusk or 8pm; ☒M41, ⑤Potsdamer Platz, ⓤPotsdamer Platz)

Checkpoint Charlie

HISTORIC SITE

2  MAP P84, E2

Checkpoint Charlie was the principal gateway for foreigners and diplomats between the two Berlins from 1961 to 1990. Unfortunately, this potent symbol of the Cold War has degenerated into a tacky tourist trap, though a free open-air exhibit that illustrates milestones in Cold War history is one redeeming aspect. (cnr Zimmerstrasse & Friedrichstrasse; admission free; ☻24hr; ⓤKochstrasse)

Topographie des Terrors

HANOHIKI/SHUTTERSTOCK ©

Gedenkstätte Deutscher Widerstand MEMORIAL

3 MAP P84, A2

This memorial exhibit on German Nazi resistance occupies the very rooms where high-ranking officers led by Claus Schenk Graf von Stauffenberg plotted the assassination attempt on Hitler on 20 July 1944. There's a memorial in the courtyard where the main conspirators were shot right after the failed coup, a story retold in the 2008 movie *Valkyrie*. (German Resistance Memorial Centre; ☏030-2699 5000; www.gdw-berlin.de; Stauffenbergstrasse 13-14; admission free; ⏱9am-6pm Mon-Fri, 10am-6pm Sat & Sun; 🚌200, M29, M48, M85, Ⓢ Potsdamer Platz, Ⓤ Potsdamer Platz, Kurfürstenstrasse)

Gropius Bau GALLERY

4 MAP P84, D2

With its mosaics, terracotta reliefs and airy atrium, this Italian Renaissance–style exhibit space named for its architect (Bauhaus founder Walter Gropius' great-uncle) is a celebrated venue for high-calibre art and cultural exhibits. Whether it's a David Bowie retrospective, the latest works of Ai Weiwei or an ethnological exhibit on the mysteries of Angkor Wat, it's bound to be well curated and engrossing. (☏030-254 860; www.gropiusbau.de; Niederkirchner Strasse 7; adult/concession/under 16yr €15/10/free; ⏱10am-7pm Fri-Wed, to 9pm Thu; Ⓟ; 🚌M41, Ⓢ Potsdamer Platz, Ⓤ Potsdamer Platz)

Berlinische Galerie GALLERY

5 MAP P84, F3

This gallery in a converted glass warehouse is a superb spot for taking stock of Berlin's art scene since 1870. Downstairs, temporary exhibits highlight contemporary artists and trends, often in unconventional or even controversial fashion. Two cross-over floating staircases lead upstairs to the permanent exhibit, with canvas candy from such art-world rock stars as Otto Dix, Jeanne Mammen and Georg Baselitz. (Berlin Museum of Modern Art, Photography & Architecture; ☏030-7890 2600; www.berlinischegalerie.de; Alte Jakobstrasse 124-128; adult/concession/child under 18yr €12/9/free; ⏱10am-6pm Wed-Mon; Ⓤ Hallesches Tor, Kochstrasse)

Berlin Story Bunker MUSEUM

6 MAP P84, C3

The multimedia exhibit 'Hitler – how could it happen', atmospherically set on three floors inside a WWII air-raid shelter, does a thorough job of documenting Hitler's rise and his impact on Germany and the world. A highlight is the 1:25 scale model of the bunker where Hitler committed suicide. Located in the same building is the **Berlin Story Museum**, which chronicles milestones in city history in a one-hour audio tour. (☏030-2655 5546; www.berlinstory.de; Schöneberger Strasse 23a; adult/concession Hitler exhibit €12/9, Berlin Story Museum €6/4.50; ⏱10am-7pm, last entry 5.30pm; 🚌M29, M41, Ⓢ Anhalter Bahnhof)

The
Berlin Wall

It's more than a tad ironic that one of Berlin's most popular tourist attractions is one that no longer exists. For 28 years the Berlin Wall, the most potent symbol of the Cold War, divided not only a city but the world.

The Beginning

Shortly after midnight on 13 August 1961, East German soldiers and police began rolling out miles of barbed wire that would soon be replaced with prefabricated concrete slabs. The Wall was a desperate measure launched by the German Democratic Republic (GDR) government to stop the sustained brain and brawn drain the country had experienced since its 1949 founding. Some 3.6 million people had already headed to western Germany, putting the GDR on the brink of economic and political collapse.

The Physical Border

Euphemistically called the 'Anti-Fascist Protection Barrier', the Berlin Wall was continually reinforced and refined. It eventually grew into a complex border-security system consisting of two walls enclosing a 'death strip' riddled with trenches, floodlights, attack dogs, electrified alarm fences and watchtowers staffed by guards with shoot-to-kill orders. Nearly 100,000 GDR citizens tried to escape, many using spectacular contraptions like homemade hot-air balloons or U-boats. There are no exact numbers, but it is believed that hundreds died in the process.

The End

The Wall's demise came as unexpectedly as its creation. Once again the GDR was losing its people in droves, this time via Hungary, which had opened its borders with Austria. Major demonstrations in East Berlin came to a head in early November 1989 when half a million people gathered on Alexanderplatz. Something had to give. It did on 9 November, when a GDR spokesperson mistakenly announced during a press conference on live TV that all travel restrictions to the West would be lifted immediately. Amid scenes of wild partying, the two Berlins came together again. Today, only about 2km of the hated barrier still stands, most famously the 1.3km-long East Side Gallery. In addition, a double row of cobblestones embedded in the pavement and 32 information panels guide visitors along 5.7km of the Wall's course through central Berlin.

Potsdamer Platz

Kulturforum Museums

In addition to the famous Gemäldegalerie (p74) and Neue Nationalgalerie (which reopened in 2021 after a five-year renovation), the Kulturforum encompasses three other top-rated museums: the **Kupferstichkabinett** (Museum of Prints & Drawings; Map p84, A2; ☎030-266 424 242; www.smb.museum/kk; Matthäikirchplatz; adult/concession €6/3; ☺10am-6pm Tue, Wed & Fri, to 8pm Thu, 11am-6pm Sat & Sun; ☐200, 300, M29, M41, M48, M85, Ⓢ Potsdamer Platz, Ⓤ Potsdamer Platz), with prints and drawings dating from the 14th century; the **Musikinstrumenten-Museum** (Musical Instruments Museum; Map p84, B1; ☎030-2548 1178; www.simpk.de; Tiergartenstrasse 1; adult/concession/under 18yr €6/3/free; ☺9am-5pm Tue, Wed & Fri, to 8pm Thu, 10am-5pm Sat & Sun), with rare historical instruments; and the **Kunstgewerbemuseum** (Museum of Decorative Arts; Map p84, A1; ☎030-266 424 242; www.smb.museum; Matthäikirchplatz; adult/concession/under 18yr €8/4/free; ☺10am-6pm Tue-Fri, 11am-6pm Sat & Sun), with its prized collection of arts and crafts. A day ticket valid for all Kulturforum museums costs €16.

Eating

Joseph-Roth-Diele   GERMAN €

7 ✖ MAP P84, A3

Named for an Austrian-Jewish writer, this wood-panelled salon time warps you back to the 1920s, when Roth used to live next door. Walls decorated with bookshelves and quotations from his works draw a literary, chatty crowd, especially at lunchtime, when two daily-changing €5.95 specials (one vegetarian) supplement the hearty menu of German classics. Pay at the counter. (☎030-2636 9884; www.joseph-roth-diele.de; Potsdamer Strasse 75; mains €8-14; ☺10am-11pm Mon-Thu, to midnight Fri; Ⓤ Kurfürstenstrasse)

Rocket + Basil   MIDDLE EASTERN €

8 ✖ MAP P84, A3

Rocket and Basil are the pets of Sophia and Xenia, German-Iranian sisters who grew up in Australia and now regale curious diners with their next-gen take on Persian cooking. Made-with-love salads, sandwiches, *khoresht* (stews) and classics like *fesenjan* (pomegranate chicken) are a Technicolor riot on the plate and flavour bursts on the palate. (☎0176 6176 7845; www.rocketandbasil.com; Lützowstrasse 22; mains €6-15; ☺11am-9pm Tue-Fri, 9am-9pm Sat, 9am-4pm Sun)

Malakeh

SYRIAN €€

9  MAP P84, A4

Malakeh Jazmati's eclectic dining room is as welcoming as a hug from an old friend. The self-taught chef from Damascus had her own TV food show in Jordan before decamping to Berlin in 2015. Now she feeds her feistily flavoured soul food to Berliners, homesick Syrians and clued-in tourists. We heartily recommend the yoghurt-based lamb stew *shakrieh*. No alcohol. (📞0176 2216 0998; Potsdamer Strasse 153; dishes €12-22; 🕑3-11pm Tue-Fri, noon-11pm Sat & Sun; 🥗; Ⓤ Bülowstrasse)

Ki-Nova

INTERNATIONAL €€

10  MAP P84, B1

The name of this lunchtime favourite hints at the concept: 'ki' is Japanese for energy and 'nova' Latin for new. 'New energy' in this case translates into health-focused yet comforting bites starring global and regional ingredients. The contemporary interior radiates urban warmth, with heavy plank tables, a black-tiled bar, movie stills and floor-to-ceiling windows. (📞030-2546 4860; www.ki-nova.de; Potsdamer Strasse 2; mains €9-15; 🕑11.30am-10pm Mon-Fri, noon-10pm Sat; 📶🥗; 🚌200, 300, M41, Ⓤ Potsdamer Platz, Ⓢ Potsdamer Platz)

Berliner Philharmoniker (p91)

CLAUDIO DIVIZIA/SHUTTERSTOCK © ARCHITECT: HANS SCHAROUN

Kin Dee

THAI €€€

11 🍴 MAP P84, A3

Kin Dee's opening created an instant buzz in 2017 and it took only two years for the Michelin testers to give it a star. Owner-chef Dalad Kambhu fearlessly catapults classic Thai dishes into the 21st century, often by using locally grown ingredients. The menu consists of eight to 10 sharing dishes, giving you maximum exposure to her creativity. (📞 030-215 5294; www.kindeeberlin.com; Lützowstrasse 81; tasting menu €65; 🕙 6-10pm Tue-Sat; 🛜; Ⓤ Kurfürstenstrasse)

Irma La Douce

FRENCH €€€

12 🍴 MAP P84, A4

Although named for the 'hooker with a heart of gold' heroine in a Billy Wilder comedy, there's nothing shady about Irma La Douce. At this brasserie near Potsdamer Platz, a glass of champagne is the overture to a symphony of next-gen French cuisine served in a sensuous 1920s-style setting. Expect plenty of unconventional flavour pairings, impeccable service and sublime wines. (📞 030-2300 0555; www.irmaladouce.de; Potsdamer Strasse 102; mains €28-43; 🕙 6-10pm; 🚌 M48, M85, Ⓤ Kurfürstenstrasse)

Layla

MIDDLE EASTERN €€€

13 🍴 MAP P84, D4

Israeli star chef Meir Adoni's fine-casual Berlin haunt takes your taste buds on a wild ride with its richly nuanced postmodern mash-up of European and Middle Eastern dishes. The sharing-is-caring concept is perfect for loading up on Yemenite brioche, smoked-aubergine carpaccio, spicy Lebanese pancakes and other treats streaming from the open kitchen. (📞 0151 2256 3654; www.layla-restaurant.com; Möckernstrasse, cnr Hallesche Strasse; 6 sharing dishes per person €55; 🕙 6-10pm Fri & Sat; Ⓢ Anhalter Bahnhof)

Drinking

Barn

COFFEE

14 ☕ MAP P84, C2

One of Berlin's most prominent third-wave coffee shops, the Barn serves its single-origin java plus coffee-based cocktails in the hallowed halls of the historic Haus Huth at Potsdamer Platz. Note the granite bar, the floating oak bench and the Eames chairs. (www.thebarn.de; Alte Potsdamer Strasse 5; 🕙 10am-5pm; 🚌 200, 300, M41, Ⓤ Potsdamer Platz, Ⓢ Potsdamer Platz)

Victoria Bar

COCKTAIL BAR

15 ☕ MAP P84, A4

Original art decorates this discreet cocktail lounge whose motto is the 'Pleasure of Serious Drinking'. It's favoured by a grown-up, artsy crowd. If you want to feel like an insider, order the off-menu 'Hilde' (vodka and champagne), created in memory of German singer-actor Hildegard Knef. (📞 030-2575 9977; www.victoriabar.de; Potsdamer Strasse 102; 🕙 6pm-late; Ⓤ Kurfürstenstrasse)

Solar Lounge
BAR

16 MAP P84, D3

Watch the city light up from this 17th-floor glass-walled sky lounge above a posh restaurant. With its dim lighting, leather couches, giant swings and breathtaking panorama, it's a great spot for sunset drinks or a date night. Getting there aboard an exterior glass lift is half the fun. The entrance is behind the Pit Stop auto shop. (📞0163 765 2700; www.solar-berlin.de; Stresemannstrasse 76; ⏰6pm-2am Thu-Sat; Ⓢ Anhalter Bahnhof)

Entertainment

Berliner Philharmoniker
CLASSICAL MUSIC

17 ⭐ MAP P84, B1

One of the world's most famous orchestras, the Berliner Philharmoniker is based at the Berliner Philharmonie, Hans Scharoun's iconic 1960s building whose unusual shape makes for optimal acoustics. Kirill Petrenko has been chief conductor since 2018. (📞 tickets 030-2548 8999; www.berliner-philharmoniker.de; Herbert-von-Karajan-Strasse 1; tickets €25-138; 🚌200, 300, M41, M29, M48, M85, Ⓢ Potsdamer Platz, Ⓤ Potsdamer Platz)

Shopping

Frau Tonis Parfum
PERFUME

18 🔒 MAP P84, E2

Follow your nose to this scent-sational made-in-Berlin perfume

Free Lunchtime Concerts

At 1pm on Tuesday from September to mid-June, the foyer of the **Berliner Philharmonie** fills with music lovers for free lunchtime chamber-music concerts. Come early for a chair or otherwise hunker down on the stairs or on the floor. Refreshments available.

boutique, where a 'scent test' reveals if you're the floral, fruity, woody or oriental type, to help you choose a matching fragrance. (📞030-2021 5310; www.frau-tonis-parfum.com; Zimmerstrasse 13; ⏰10am-6pm Mon-Sat; Ⓤ Kochstrasse)

Mall of Berlin
MALL

19 🔒 MAP P84, C1

This sparkling retail quarter is tailor-made for black-belt mall rats. More than 270 shops vie for your euros, including flagship stores by Karl Lagerfeld, Hugo Boss, Liebeskind, Marc Cain, Muji and other international high-end brands, alongside the usual high-street chains like Mango and H&M. Kids love the giant indoor slide on the 2nd floor. (www.mallofberlin.de; Leipziger Platz 12; ⏰10am-8pm Mon-Sat; 🛜♿; 🚌200, 300, M48, Ⓤ Potsdamer Platz, Ⓢ Potsdamer Platz)

Explore ◈
Hackescher Markt & Scheunenviertel

The Scheunenviertel (Barn Quarter) packs plenty of charisma into its compact size and is fun to explore by day and night. Walking around you'll constantly stumble upon enchanting surprises: here an idyllic courtyard or bleeding-edge gallery, there a fashion-forward boutique or belle-époque ballroom. Since reunification, the area has also reprised its historic role as Berlin's main Jewish quarter.

The Short List

○ **Gedenkstätte Berliner Mauer (p94)** *Coming to grips with the absurdity of a divided city at this Berlin Wall memorial exhibit.*

○ **Hackesche Höfe (p98)** *Exploring fashion boutiques, shops, galleries and cafes in this charismatic courtyard maze.*

○ **Neue Synagoge (p99)** *Admiring the exotic architecture and studying up on the quarter's Jewish history.*

○ **KW Institute for Contemporary Art (p99)** *Keeping tabs on the latest developments in the art world.*

Getting There & Around

Ⓤ Weinmeisterstrasse (U8) is the most central station. For Torstrasse, get off at Rosenthaler Platz (U8), Rosa-Luxemburg-Platz (U2) or Oranienburger Tor (U6).

Ⓢ Hackescher Markt (S5, S7, S75) and Oranienburger Strasse (S1, S2, S25) stations are both good jumping-off points.

🚊 M1 runs from Museumsinsel (Museum Island) to Prenzlauer Berg and stops throughout the Scheunenviertel.

Neighbourhood Map on p96

Neue Synagoge (p99) FHM/GETTY IMAGES ©

Top Experience 📷

Take in History at the Gedenkstätte Berliner Mauer

For an insightful primer on the Berlin Wall, visit this 1.4km-long outdoor memorial, which explains the physical layout of the barrier and the death strip, how the border fortifications were enlarged and perfected over time, and what impact they had on the daily lives of people on both sides of the Wall. The exhibit follows Bernauer Strasse, which was once divided by the Wall.

◎ MAP P96, C2

www.berliner-mauer-gedenkstaette.de

🕐 visitor & documentation centre 10am-6pm Thu-Sun, open-air exhibit 8am-10pm

Ⓢ Nordbahnhof, Bernauer Strasse

National Monument to German Division

Near Ackerstrasse the central memorial to German division consists of a 70m section of original wall bounded by two rusted steel flanks. Through gaps in the inner wall, you can glimpse a reconstructed death strip complete with a guard tower, a security patrol path and the lamps that bathed it in fierce light at night.

Dokumentationszentrum

Across the street from the national monument, the documentation centre provides a concise and engaging overview of the Wall and answers such questions as to why it was built and what led to its collapse. It also uses artefacts, documents and videos to show how it affected daily life on both sides.

Window of Remembrance

Between Gartenstrasse and Ackerstrasse, a wall of photographic portraits gives identity to would-be escapees who lost their lives at the Berlin Wall, one of them only six years old (pictured).

Kapelle der Versöhnung

The modern Chapel of Reconciliation stands in the spot of an 1894 brick church detonated in 1985 to make room for a widening of the border strip. A 15-minute remembrance service for Wall victims is held at noon Tuesday to Friday.

Nordbahnhof 'Ghost Station'

The wall also divided the city's transport system. Three lines that originated in West Berlin had to travel along tracks that happened to run beneath East Berlin before returning to stations back on the western side. Trains slowed down but did not stop at these so-called 'ghost stations'. S-Bahn station Nordbahnhof has an exhibit on the subject.

★ Top Tips

o Start your visit in the visitor centre across from Nordbahnhof S-Bahn station and work your way east.

o Pick up a free map and watch the introductory film at the visitor centre.

o For a self-guided tour, go to www. berliner-mauer.mobi.

o If you have limited time, spend it in the first section between Gartenstrasse and Ackerstrasse.

✗ Take a Break

o **Castle** (☑0151 6767 6757; www.thecastle berlin.de; Invalidenstrasse 129; ☺2pm-1am Mon-Thu, 2pm-2am Fri, 1pm-1am Sun; 🛜; 🚌M5, M8, M10, 12, 🇸Nordbahnhof) is a fine place for coffee and pastries before and craft beer after your sightseeing (or vice versa). Free wi-fi and beer garden.

A **B** **C** **D**

1

For reviews see
- ◉ Top Experiences p94
- ◉ Sights p98
- ✖ Eating p100
- 🍷 Drinking p103
- ★ Entertainment p104
- 🔒 Shopping p105

Bernauer Str

Strelitzer Str

2

Chausseestr

Habersaathstr

Bergstr

Ackerstr

Gedenkstätte Berliner Mauer ◉

Gartenstr

Bergstr

Bernauer Str

Nordbahnhof Ⓢ

Invalidenstr

13 ✖

Bergstr

Naturkundemuseum Ⓤ

Museum für Naturkunde ◉ 3

3

Invalidenstr

Eichendorffstr

Schlegelstr

Chausseestr

Tieckstr

Novalisstr

Gartenstr

Hamburger Bahnhof – Museum für Gegenwart ◀◉ 2

Hannoversche Str

4

Luisenstr

Hannoversche Str

Torstr

12 ✖
✖ **16**

KW Institute for Contemporary Art ◉ 6

Linienstr

Oranienburger Ⓤ **Tor**

Oranienburger Str

Auguststr

Humboldt-Universität zu Berlin

5

Friedrichstr

Oranienburger Ⓢ **Str**

24 🔒
Heckmann Höfe
11 ✖
5 ◉
Neue Synagoge

✖ **9**

Johannisstr

Kalkscheunenstr

Tucholskystr

Monbijoustr

Sammlung Boros ◉ 4

★ **23**

Reinhardtstr

Ziegelstr

Schumannstr

6

Luisenstr

Albrechtstr

Marienstr

Spree River
Am Weidendamm

Ⓤ

A **B** **C** **D**

E **F** **G** **H**

0 ——— 400 m
0 ——— 0.2 miles

Brunnenstr

Anklamer Str

Swinemünder Str

Zionskirchplatz

Kastanienallee

Fehrbelliner Str

Chroiner Str

Schwedter Str

Veteranenstr

18 🍴 Weinbergsweg

17 🍴

Weinbergspark

Senefelderplatz

Teutoburger
Platz

Ackerstr

Brunnenstr

7 ⊙ Times
Art Center Berlin

Rosenthaler
Platz

10 Ⓤ

🍴 20

Torstr

Torstr

Schönhauser Allee

14 ✕

Koppenplatz

Linienstr

Rosenthaler Str

Linienstr

Rosa-
Luxemburg-
Platz

Ⓤ

27 🔒 ✕ 8

15 ✕

Grosse Hamburger Str

Sophienstr

Augustr

Gipsstr

Gormannstr

Mulackstr

Steinstr

Alte Schönhauser Str

Max-Beer-Str

Almstadtstr

Rosa-Luxemburg Str

Weydinger
Str

21 🏛

Hirtenstr

25 🔒

26 🔒 Weinmeisterstr

Ⓤ

Krausnickstr

Friedhof Grosse
Hamburger
Strasse

19 🏛
22 ⊙ 1 ⊙

Neue
Schönhauser Str

Weinmeisterstr

Haus Schwarzenberg
Hackesche
Höfe

Münzstr

Karl-Liebknecht-Str

Oranienburger Str

Monbijou
Park

Monbijouplatz

Grosse Präsidentenstr

Neue Promenade

Dircksenstr

Rochstr

James-
Simon-
Park

E **F** **G** **H**

Sights

Hackesche Höfe
HISTORIC SITE

1 ◉ MAP P96, F5

The Hackesche Höfe is the largest and most famous of the courtyard ensembles peppered throughout the Scheunenviertel. Built in 1907, the eight interlinked *Höfe* reopened in 1996 with a congenial mix of cafes, galleries, shops and entertainment venues. The main entrance on Rosenthaler Strasse leads to **Court I**, prettily festooned with art-nouveau tiles, while Court VII segues to the romantic **Rosenhöfe** with a sunken rose garden and tendril-like balustrades. Enter from Rosenthaler Strasse 40/41 or Sophienstrasse 6. (Hackesche Courtyards; ☎030-2809 8010; www.hackesche-hoefe.com; ☒M1, Ⓢ Hackescher Markt, Ⓤ Weinmeisterstrasse)

Hamburger Bahnhof – Museum für Gegenwart
MUSEUM

2 ◉ MAP P96, A4

Berlin's main contemporary-art museum opened in 1996 in a mid-19th-century railway station, whose late-neoclassical grandeur is an impressive backdrop for this profusion of paintings, installations, sculptures and video art. Changing exhibits span the arc of post-1950 artistic movements – from conceptual art and pop art to minimal art and Fluxus – and include seminal works by such major players as Andy Warhol, Cy Twombly, Joseph Beuys and Robert Rauschenberg. (☎030-266 424 242; www.smb.museum; Invalidenstrasse 50-51; adult/concession/under 18yr €10/5/free, 4-8pm 1st Thu of month free; ⏰10am-6pm Tue, Wed & Fri, to 8pm Thu, 11am-6pm Sat & Sun; ☒M5, M6, M8, M10, Ⓢ Hauptbahnhof, Ⓤ Hauptbahnhof)

Museum für Naturkunde
MUSEUM

3 ◉ MAP P96, A3

Fossils and minerals don't quicken your pulse? Well, how about a 13m-high Giraffatitan skeleton, the superstar among the Jurassic lineup at this highly engaging museum in a gorgeous building. Elsewhere you can wave at Knut, the world's most famous dead polar bear; marvel at the fragile bones of an ultra-rare Archaeopteryx protobird; and find out why zebras are striped. (Museum of Natural History; ☎030-8891 408 591; www.museum fuernaturkunde.berlin; Invalidenstrasse 43; adult/concession incl audioguide €8/5; ⏰9.30am-6pm Tue-Fri, 10am-6pm Sat & Sun; ♿; ☒M5, M8, M10, 12, Ⓤ Naturkundemuseum)

Sammlung Boros
GALLERY

4 ◉ MAP P96, B6

A Nazi-era bunker serves as the backdrop to the Sammlung Boros, the sublime private collection of contemporary art amassed by advertising guru Christian Boros, who acquired the behemoth in 2003. Selections change every few years and currently include installations by Katja Novitskova, digital paintings by Avery Singer and photo series by Peter Piller. Book online (weeks, if not months, ahead) to join a guided tour (also in English) and to pick up fascinating nuggets about the building's surprising other peacetime incarnations. (Boros Collection; www.sammlung-boros.de; Reinhardtstrasse 20; adult/concession €18/10; ⏱10am-6.30pm Fri-Sun; 🚊M1, Ⓢ Friedrichstrasse, Ⓤ Oranienburger Tor, Friedrichstrasse)

Neue Synagoge SYNAGOGUE

5 ◉ MAP P96, D5

The gleaming gold dome of the Neue Synagoge is the most visible symbol of Berlin's revitalised Jewish community. The 1866 original was Germany's largest synagogue at the time, but its modern incarnation is not so much a house of worship (although prayer services do take place) as a museum and place of remembrance called Centrum Judaicum. (☏030-8802 8300; www.centrumjudaicum.de; Oranienburger Strasse 28-30; adult/concession €7/4.50, audioguide €3; ⏱10am-6pm Mon-Fri, to 7pm Sun Apr-Sep, 10am-6pm Sun-Thu, 10am-3pm Fri Oct-Mar; 🚊M1, Ⓤ Oranienburger Tor, Ⓢ Oranienburger Strasse)

KW Institute for Contemporary Art GALLERY

6 ◉ MAP P96, D4

Founded in the early 1990s in an old margarine factory, nonprofit KW played a key role in turning the Scheunenviertel into Berlin's first major post-Wall art district.

Hackesche Höfe

KIEV.VICTOR/SHUTTERSTOCK ©

Hackescher Markt & Scheunenviertel Sights

Haus Schwarzenberg

Haus Schwarzenberg (Map p96, F5; www.haus-schwarzenberg.org; Rosenthaler Strasse 39; admission free; ⏱courtyard 24hr; 🚋M1, ⑤Hackescher Markt) is the last holdout in the heavily gentrified area around the Hackescher Markt. Run by a nonprofit organisation, it's an unpretentious space where art and creativity are allowed to flourish beyond the mainstream and commerce. Festooned with street art and bizarre metal sculptures, the courtyards lead to studios, offices, the underground 'amusement park' **Monsterkabinett**, the edgy-arty **Eschschloraque Rümschrümp** bar, an art-house cinema – outdoors in summer – and a couple of small **museums** dealing with Jewish persecution during the Third Reich.

It continues to stage boundary-pushing exhibits that reflect the latest – and often radical – trends in contemporary art. (📞030-243 4590; www.kw-berlin.de; Auguststrasse 69; adult/concession €8/6, 6-9pm Thu free; ⏱11am-7pm Mon, Wed & Fri-Sun, to 9pm Thu; 🚋M1, ⑤Oranienburger Strasse, Ⓤ Oranienburger Tor)

Times Art Center Berlin

GALLERY

 7 MAP P96, F3

Contemporary Chinese art has thus far pretty much flown under the radar in Western countries, a shortcoming the private, nonprofit Guangzhou Times Art Museum set out to change by opening its first European branch in Berlin in 2018. On three suitably austere floors, curators mount several boundary-pushing shows annually, with a focus on multimedia and video art. (📞030-2478 1038; www.timesart center.org; Brunnenstrasse 9; admission free; ⏱noon-7pm Tue-Sat)

Eating

KWA

MIDDLE EASTERN €

 8 MAP P96, E4

Kebab with Attitude has upped the ante in the Berlin *Döner* stakes by using only free-range, sustainable beef and chicken and hand-stacking it onto the giant skewer. Skip the fancy versions with mango or truffle and keep it classic with crisp cabbage and salad. Excellent homemade sauces and *ayran* (Turkish yoghurt drink). Conclusion: pricey but worth it. (📞030-3552 9966; www.eatkwa.de; Gipsstrasse 2; mains €8-17; ⏱noon-10pm Sun-Thu, to 11pm Fri & Sat; Ⓤ Rosenthaler Platz, Weinmeisterstrasse)

House of Small Wonder

FUSION €

9 MAP P96, C5

A wrought-iron staircase spirals up to this day-to-night oasis where potted plants and whimsical decor create a relaxed backyard-garden feel. The food is mostly Japanese riffs on international comfort food, like the *mentaiko* spaghetti, the millefeuille *katsu* or the Okinawan taco rice. Also a popular spot for brunch or just coffee and home-baked pastries like the matcha roulade. (📞030-2758 2877; www.houseofsmallwonder.de; Johannisstrasse 20; mains €8-21; ⏰9am-10pm; �📶🌱; Ⓤ Oranienburger Tor, Ⓢ Oranienburger Strasse, Friedrichstrasse)

Rosenthaler Grill und Schlemmerbuffet MIDDLE EASTERN €

10 🍴 MAP P96, F3

Veteran family-run *Döner* and ke-bab joint with homemade sauces and bread, indoor-outdoor seating and nonstop service for early birds, night owls and everyone in-between. Also does respectable grilled chicken and pizza. (📞030-283 2153; www.rosenthaler-grill.de; Torstrasse 125; dishes €3-8; ⏰24hr; 🚋M1, 12, Ⓤ Rosenthaler Platz)

Tadshikische Teestube RUSSIAN €

11 🍴 MAP P96, D5

Treat yourself to a Russian tea ceremony complete with silvery samovar, biscuits and vodka, or tuck into hearty Russian *blini* (pancakes) or *vareniki* (dumplings) while reclining amid plump pillows, hand-carved sandalwood pillars and heroic murals in this original Tajik tearoom. The authentic space was gifted by the Soviets to the East German government in 1974. Cash only.

In summer the sun-dappled courtyard is a mellow spot for a bite or drink. (📞030-204 1112; www.tadshikische-teestube.de; KunstHof, Oranienburger Strasse 27; mains €7-12; ⏰4-11pm Mon-Fri, noon-11pm Sat & Sun; 🚋M1, Ⓢ Oranienburger Strasse)

Frea VEGAN €€

12 🍴 MAP P96, D4

As a completely vegan and zero-waste restaurant, Frea pushes new boundaries in ethical and ultra-sustainable eating. From sourdough bread to chocolate, everything's made in-house from regional ingredients; food scraps are composted and returned to the growers as fertiliser. Dishes like pumpkin-potato-filled agnolotti may be modest in size but pack a big flavour punch. (📞030-9839 6198; www.frea.de; Torstrasse 180; mains €17-18; ⏰5.30pm-midnight; 🌱; 🚋142, Ⓤ Rosenthaler Platz)

Katz Orange INTERNATIONAL €€

13 🍴 MAP P96, D3

With its thoughtful farm-to-table menu, stylish country flair and top-notch cocktails, the 'Orange Cat' hits a gastro grand slam. It will have you purring for such perennial favourites as Duroc pork that's been slow-roasted for 12 hours (nicknamed 'candy on bone'). The setting in a castle-like former brewery is stunning, especially in summer when the patio opens. (📞030-983 208 430; www.katzorange.com; Bergstrasse 22; mains €18-25; ⏰6-11pm; 🚋M8, Ⓤ Rosenthaler Platz)

Kopps

VEGAN €€

14 MAP P96, E4

If you're in the mood for plant-based fine dining, call the Kopps! From turnips to carrots, the cosmo-comfy Scheunenviertel kitchen has been coaxing maximum flavour out of the vegetable kingdom long before vegan went mainstream. The beautiful nosh is matched by a wine list heavy on natural and organic bottles. Loyal locals practically mob the place on weekends for brunch. (📞030-4320 9775; www.kopps-berlin.de; Linienstrasse 94; 3-course lunch €15, 3-course dinner menu €48, additional courses €8, 4-course brunch €25; ⏱noon-2pm & 5.30-9.30pm Sun-Thu, 5.30-10.30pm Fri & Sat; 🖋; 🚊M1, Ⓤ Rosenthaler Platz)

Clärchens Ballhaus

GERMAN €€

15 MAP P96, E5

The glitter walls are gone and so are the beloved cross-generational dance parties. Since Clärchens changed owners in 2019, the venerable early-20th-century ballroom has mostly become a restaurant serving modern reinterpretations of traditional Berlin cuisine as well as Sunday brunch in the charmingly morbid Spiegelsaal (Mirror Hall) upstairs. In summer, the beer garden beckons. (📞030-555 785 440; https://claerchensball.haus; Auguststrasse 24; mains €11-22; ⏱5-11pm Mon-Thu & Sun, 5pm-1am Fri, noon-1am Sat; 🚊M1, Ⓢ Oranienburger Strasse)

Stolpersteine

MATIAS PLANAS/SHUTTERSTOCK ©

Stumbling upon History

If you lower your gaze you'll see them all over town, but nowhere are they more concentrated than in the Scheunenviertel: small brass paving stones in front of house entrances. Called **Stolpersteine** (stumbling blocks), they are part of a nationwide project by Berlin-born artist Gunter Demnig and are essentially mini-memorials honouring the people (usually Jews) who lived in the respective houses before being killed by the Nazis. The engravings indicate the person's name, birth year, year of deportation, the name of the concentration camp where they were taken and the date they perished.

Schwarzwaldstuben   GERMAN €€

 16   MAP P96, D4

Fancy a 'Hansel and Gretel' moment? Join the other 'lost kids' for satisfying slow food from the southwest German regions of Baden and Swabia. Tuck into gut-filling plates of *Kässpätzle* (mac 'n' cheese), *Maultaschen* (ravioli-like pasta), crispy *Flammkuchen* (Alsatian pizza) or a giant schnitzel with fried potatoes. Dine inside amid rustic forest decor or grab a sidewalk table. Cash only. (☏030-2809 8084; www.schwarzwaldstuben-berlin.com; Tucholskystrasse 48; mains €7.50-19.50; ⏱noon-midnight Mon-Fri, 9am-11pm Sat & Sun; ☐M1, Ⓢ Oranienburger Strasse, Ⓤ Oranienburger Tor)

Drinking

Buck & Breck   COCKTAIL BAR

17   MAP P96, E3

Liquid maestro Gonçalo de Sousa Monteiro and his baseball-cap-wearing team treat grown-up patrons to libational flights of fancy in their clandestine cocktail salon with sophisticated yet friendly flair. Historical short drinks are a strength, including the eponymous bubbly-based cocktail Buck and Breck, named for mid-19th-century US president James Buchanan and his VP John Breckinridge. (☏0176 3231 5507; Brunnenstrasse 177; ⏱7pm-4am; ☐M1, Ⓤ Rosenthaler Platz)

Rosengarten   BEER GARDEN

18   MAP P96, F3

Hemmed in by roses, this little outdoor bar/beer garden in a pavilion at the edge of the Weinbergspark, opposite Weinbergsweg 13, doles out cocktails and culture to a chilled, eclectic crowd in the warmer months. Run by a nonprofit, it's a tradition going back to the 19th century. (www.rosengarten-berlin.de; ⏱3-10pm or later Mon-Fri, noon-10pm or later Sat & Sun Apr-Sep; ☐M1, M13, Ⓤ Rosenthaler Platz)

Eschschloraque Rümschrümp

BAR

19 🗺 MAP P96, F5

A project by the artists collective Dead Chickens, this subculture survivor is filled with metal monster sculptures and hosts concerts, parties and performance art beyond the mainstream – from Dada burlesque to Balkan post-punk concerts. Small beer garden.

It's in the last courtyard of the street-art-festooned Haus Schwarzenberg (p100). (www.eschschloraque.de; Haus Schwarzenberg, 2nd courtyard, Rosenthaler Strasse 39; ⏱6pm-1am Sun-Tue, 3pm-1am Wed-Sat; 🚋M1, 🚈Hackescher Markt)

Mikkeler

CRAFT BEER

20 🗺 MAP P96, F4

Mikkeler – the name stands for Mikkel Borg Bjergsø and Kristian Klarup Keller – dispenses elevated craft beer that the two Danes have been brewing since 2006. In their first beer salon in Germany, their two dozen signature and guest brews on tap are best enjoyed over free-flowing conversation at the bar amid minimalist Scandinavian-woodsy surroundings. (☎0176 8314 1103; Torstrasse 102; ⏱5pm-midnight; 🚈Rosenthaler Platz)

Entertainment

Babylon

CINEMA

21 ⭐ MAP P96, H5

This top-rated indie screens a smart line-up of cinematic expression, from experimental German films and international art-house flicks to themed retrospectives and other stuff you'd never catch at the multiplex. For silent movies, including a free show at midnight on Saturday, the historic theatre organ is put through its paces. Also hosts film festivals, readings and concerts. (☎030-242 5969; www.babylonberlin.de; Rosa-Luxemburg-Strasse 30; tickets €7-10; 🚈Rosa-Luxemburg-Platz)

Chamäleon

CABARET

22 ⭐ MAP P96, F5

A marriage of art-nouveau charms and high-tech theatre trappings, this intimate venue in a 1920s-style ballroom is a prime address for sophisticated 'contemporary circus' shows. This translates into a blend of comedy, acrobatics, music, juggling and dance – often in sassy, sexy and unconventional fashion. Sit at the bar, at bistro tables or in comfy armchairs. (☎030-400 0590; www.chamaeleonberlin.com; Rosenthaler Strasse 40/41; tickets €37-59; 🚋M1, M4, M5, M6, 🚈Hackescher Markt, 🚈Weinmeisterstrasse)

Friedrichstadt-Palast Berlin

PERFORMING ARTS

23 ⭐ MAP P96, C5

Europe's largest revue theatre has been putting on the glitz for well over a century. Night after night its huge ensemble delights audiences with visually stunning Vegas-style shows featuring leggy dancers, singing, stunning costuming, a high-tech stage and fabulous special effects and artistry. Productions are innovative and highly entertaining, and don't require German skills. (☑030-2326 2326; www.palast.berlin; Friedrichstrasse 107; tickets €20-190; �🚊M1, ⓤOranienburger Tor, ⓢFriedrichstrasse, Oranienburger Strasse)

Shopping

Bonbonmacherei FOOD

24 🔒 MAP P96, D5

The aroma of peppermint and liquorice wafts through this old-fashioned basement candy kitchen whose owners use antique equipment and time-tested recipes to churn out souvenir-worthy bonbons from sweet and sour to spicy. Be sure to try their signature leaf-shaped *Berliner Maiblätter*, made with woodruff. Mix and match your own bag. (☑030-4405 5243; www.bonbonmacherei.de; Heckmann Höfe, Oranienburger Strasse 32; ⊙noon-7pm Wed-Sat Sep-Jun; 🚊M1, ⓢOranienburger Strasse)

Kauf Dich Glücklich FASHION & ACCESSORIES

25 🔒 MAP P96, F5

What began as a waffle cafe and vintage shop has turned into a small emporium of indie concept boutiques, with this branch as the flagship. The rambling store presents a Berlin-eclectic mix of reasonably priced on-trend clothing, home accessories, books and cosmetics from its own KDG collection and other hand-picked labels, many from Scandinavia. (☑030-2887 8817; www.kaufdich gluecklich-shop.de; Rosenthaler Strasse 17; ⊙11am-8pm Mon-Sat; ⓤWeinmeisterstrasse)

1. Absinth Depot Berlin FOOD & DRINKS

26 🔒 MAP P96, G5

Vincent Van Gogh, Henri de Toulouse-Lautrec and Oscar Wilde are among the fin-de-siècle artists who drew inspiration from the 'green fairy', as absinthe is also known. This quaint little shop has over 100 varieties of the potent stuff and an expert owner who'll happily help you pick out the perfect bottle for your own mind-altering rendezvous. (☑030-281 6789; www.erstesabsinthdepotberlin.de; Weinmeisterstrasse 4; ⊙2pm-midnight Mon-Fri, 1pm-midnight Sat; ⓤWeinmeisterstrasse)

Do You Read Me?! BOOKS

27 🔒 MAP P96, E4

Trend chasers could probably spend hours flicking through this gallery-style assortment of cool, obscure and small-print magazines from around the world. There's a distinct focus on fashion, design, architecture, music, art and contemporary trends, and knowledgeable staff to help you navigate, if needed. (☑030-6954 9695; www.doyoureadme.de; Auguststrasse 28; ⊙10am-7.30pm Mon-Sat; 🚊M1, M5, ⓢOranienburger Strasse, ⓤRosenthaler Platz)

Explore ◈

Kurfürstendamm & City West

West Berlin's commercial hub during the city's Cold War–era division, Charlottenburg still counts its famous shopping boulevard, the Kurfürstendamm, among its biggest drawcards. Its eastern end, around the famous Zoo Berlin, has been undergoing major revitalisation, while nearby Schloss Charlottenburg is a treat for royal groupies. Leafy side streets, lined with palatial townhouses, still reflect the area's bourgeois charms.

The Short List

○ **Schloss Charlottenburg (p120)** *Marvelling at the pomposity of the Prussian royal lifestyle.*

○ **Kaiser-Wilhelm-Gedächtniskirche (p110)** *Considering the horror of war at this ruined church.*

○ **Zoo Berlin (p110)** *Communing with apes and zebras at the world's most species-rich animal park.*

○ **Bikini Berlin (p118)** *Shopping for fashion and accessories at this architecturally stunning concept mall.*

Getting There & Around

🚌 Bus 100 and 200 both depart from Zoologischer Garten. M19 and M29 travel along Kurfürstendamm. Lines 109 and M45 go to Schloss Charlottenburg.

Ⓢ S5 and S7 link to Hauptbahnhof and Alexanderplatz via Zoologischer Garten and link with the circle line S41/S42 at Westkreuz.

Ⓤ Uhlandstrasse, Kurfürstendamm and Wittenbergplatz stations (U1) put you right in shopping central. The U2 passes through Zoologischer Garten.

Neighbourhood Map on p108

Orangutan in Zoo Berlin (p110) OSCITY/SHUTTERSTOCK ©

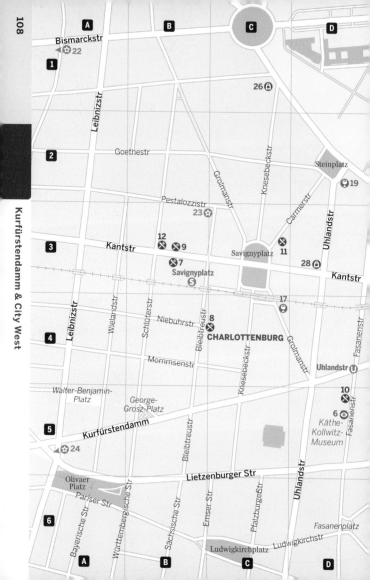

A **B** **C** **D**

Bismarckstr

☆22

1

Leibnizstr

2

Goethestr

Grolmanstr

26🔒

Steinplatz

Knesebeckstr

Carmerstr

☕19

Pestalozzistr

23☆

Uhlandstr

3

Kantstr

12
✕ ✕9

Savignyplatz

✕
11

28🔒

✕7

Kantstr

Savignyplatz
Ⓢ

17
☕

Leibnizstr

Wielandstr

Schlüterstr

Niebuhrstr

Bleibtreustr

8
✕

Grolmanstr

Fasanenstr

4

CHARLOTTENBURG

Mommsenstr

Knesebeckstr

Uhlandstr Ⓤ

Walter-Benjamin-
Platz

George-
Grosz-Platz

10
✕

Fasanenstr

6 ◉
Käthe-
Kollwitz-
Museum

5

Kurfürstendamm

Bleibtreustr

Uhlandstr

☆24

Olivaer
Platz

Bayerische Str

Württembergische Str

Pariser Str

Sächsische Str

Emser Str

Lietzenburger Str

Pfalzburger Str

Fasanenplatz

6

Ludwigkirchplatz

Ludwigkirchstr

A **B** **C** **D**

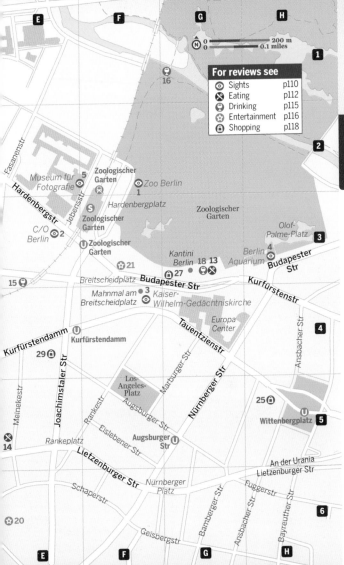

For reviews see

	Sights	p110
	Eating	p112
	Drinking	p115
	Entertainment	p116
	Shopping	p118

N 0 — 200 m
0 — 0.1 miles

16

Museum für Fotografie 5

Zoologischer Garten

Zoo Berlin 1

Hardenbergplatz

Zoologischer Garten

C/O Berlin 2

Zoologischer Garten

Hardenbergstr

Fasanenstr

Jebensstr

Zoologischer Garten

21

Kantini Berlin

18 13

27

Berlin Aquarium

Olof-Palme-Platz 3

4

Budapester Str

15

Breitscheidplatz

Budapester Str

Kurfürstenstr

Mahnmal am Breitscheidplatz

3

Kaiser-Wilhelm-Gedächtniskirche

Europa Center

Tauentzienstr

Ansbacher Str

Kurfürstendamm

Kurfürstendamm

29

Joachimstaler Str

Meinekestr

Rankestr

Los-Angeles-Platz

Augsburger Str

Marburger Str

Nürnberger Str

25

Wittenbergplatz 5

Eislebener Str

Augsburger Str

14

Rankeplatz

Lietzenburger Str

Nürnberger Platz

An der Urania

Lietzenburger Str

Fuggerstr

Schaperstr

20

Geisbergstr

Bamberger Str

Ansbacher Str

Bayreuther Str

Sights

Zoo Berlin

ZOO

1 ⊙ MAP P108, F2

Berlin's zoo holds a triple record as Germany's oldest (since 1844), most species rich and most popular animal park. Top billing at the moment goes to a pair of bamboo-devouring pandas on loan from China. The menagerie includes nearly 20,000 critters representing 1500 species, including orangutans, rhinos, giraffes and penguins. Public feeding sessions take place throughout the day – check the schedule online and by the ticket counter. (🕿030-254 010; www.zoo-berlin.de; Hardenbergplatz 8; adult/child €16/8, with aquarium €22/11; ⏱9am-6.30pm Apr-Sep, to 6pm Mar & Oct, to 4.30pm Nov-Feb, last entry 1hr before closing; 🚌100, 200, Ⓢ Zoologischer Garten, Ⓤ Zoologischer Garten, Kurfürstendamm)

C/O Berlin

GALLERY

2 ⊙ MAP P108, E3

Founded in 2000, C/O Berlin is the capital's most respected private, nonprofit exhibition centre for international photography. It is based at the iconic Amerika Haus, which served as a US cultural and information centre from 1957 until 2006. C/O's roster of highbrow exhibits regularly features the art form's international elite, including Annie Leibovitz, Stephen Shore, Nan Goldin and Anton Corbijn.

(🕿030-284 441 662; www.co-berlin.org; Hardenbergstrasse 22-24; adult/concession/child under 18yr €10/6/free; ⏱11am-8pm; Ⓟ; Ⓢ Zoologischer Garten, Ⓤ Zoologischer Garten)

Kaiser-Wilhelm-Gedächtniskirche

CHURCH

3 ⊙ MAP P108, F4

Allied bombing in 1943 left only the husk of the west tower of this once magnificent neo-Romanesque church standing. Now an antiwar memorial, it stands quiet and dignified amid the roaring traffic. Historic photographs displayed in the **Gedenkhalle** (Hall of Remembrance), in the church's former entrance hall, help you visualise the lost grandeur of this 1895 church. The adjacent octagonal hall of worship, added in 1961, has glowing midnight-blue glass walls and a giant 'floating' Jesus. (Kaiser Wilhelm Memorial Church; 🕿030-218 5023; www.gedaechtniskirche.com; Breitscheidplatz; admission free; ⏱church 10am-6pm, memorial hall noon-5.30pm; Ⓤ Zoologischer Garten, Kurfürstendamm, Ⓢ Zoologischer Garten)

Berlin Aquarium

AQUARIUM

4 ⊙ MAP P108, H3

Three floors of exotic fish, amphibians and reptiles await at this endearingly old-fashioned aquarium with its darkened halls and glowing tanks. Some of the denizens of the famous **Crocodile Hall** could be the stuff of nightmares, but dancing jellyfish, iridescent poison frogs and

Berlin in the 'Golden' Twenties

The 1920s began as anything but golden, marked by a lost war, social and political instability, hyperinflation, hunger and disease. Many Berliners responded by behaving like there was no tomorrow and made their city as much a den of decadence as a cauldron of creativity. Cabaret, Dada and jazz flourished. Pleasure pits popped up everywhere, turning the city into a 'sextropolis' of Dionysian dimensions. Bursting with energy, it became a laboratory for anything new and modern, drawing giants of architecture (Hans Scharoun, Walter Gropius), fine arts (George Grosz, Max Beckmann) and literature (Bertolt Brecht, Christopher Isherwood).

Cafes & Cabaret

Cabarets provided a titillating fantasy of play and display where cross-dressers, singers, magicians, dancers and other entertainers made audiences forget the harsh realities. Kurfürstendamm evolved into a major nightlife hub with glamorous cinemas, theatres and restaurants. The Romanisches Café, on the site of today's Europa-Center, was practically the second living room for artists, actors, writers, photographers, film producers and other creative types, some famous, most not. German writer Erich Kästner even called it the 'waiting room of the talented'.

Celluloid History

The 1920s and early '30s were also a boom time for Berlin cinema, with Marlene Dietrich seducing the world and the mighty UFA studio producing virtually all of Germany's celluloid output. Fritz Lang, whose seminal works *Metropolis* (1926) and *M* (1931) brought him international fame, was among the dominant film-makers.

The Crash

The fun came to an instant end when the US stock market crashed in 1929, plunging the world into economic depression. Within weeks, half a million Berliners were jobless, and riots and demonstrations again ruled the streets. The volatile, increasingly polarised political climate led to clashes between communists and the emerging NS-DAP (Nazi Party), led by Adolf Hitler. Soon jackboots, Brownshirts, oppression and fear would dominate daily life in Germany.

Mahnmal am Breitscheidplatz

This simple **memorial** (Map p108, F4; Breitscheidplatz; 🚌100, 200, Ⓤ Zoologischer Garten, Ⓢ Zoologischer Garten) honours the victims of the terror attack of 19 December 2016, when a man drove a truck into a crowd at the Christmas market held every year on Breitscheidplatz. Unveiled on the event's one-year anniversary, it consists of a golden crack that runs down the steps leading up to the Kaiser Wilhelm Memorial Church, with the names of the dozen victims chiselled into the front of the steps.

a real-life 'Nemo' bring smiles to young and old. (📞030-254 010; www.aquarium-berlin.de; Budapester Strasse 32; adult/child €16/8, with zoo €22/11; ⏰9am-6pm; 🚻; Ⓢ Zoologischer Garten, Ⓤ Zoologischer Garten)

Museum für Fotografie GALLERY

5 ◉ MAP P108, E2

A former Prussian officers' casino now showcases the artistic legacy of Helmut Newton (1920–2004), the Berlin-born *enfant terrible* of fashion and lifestyle photography, with the two lower floors dedicated to his life and work as well as to the artistic output of photographic compatriots, such as his wife, Alice Springs. On the top floor, the barrel-vaulted **Kaisersaal** (Emperor's Hall) forms a grand backdrop for changing international photography exhibits. (📞030-266 424 242; www.smb.museum/mf; Jebensstrasse 2; adult/concession €10/5; ⏰11am-7pm Tue, Wed & Fri-Sun, to 8pm Thu; Ⓢ Zoologischer Garten, Ⓤ Zoologischer Garten)

Käthe-Kollwitz-Museum MUSEUM

6 ◉ MAP P108, D5

Käthe Kollwitz (1867–1945) was a famous early-20th-century artist whose social and political awareness lent a tortured power to her lithographs, graphics, woodcuts, sculptures and drawings. This four-floor exhibit in a charming 19th-century villa kicks off with an introduction to this extraordinary woman, who lived in Berlin for 52 years, before presenting a life-spanning selection of her work, including the powerful anti-hunger lithography *Brot!* (Bread!, 1924) and the woodcut series *Krieg* (War, 1922–3). (📞030-882 5210; www.kaethe-kollwitz.de; Fasanenstrasse 24; adult/concession/under 18yr €7/4/free, audioguide €3; ⏰11am-4pm; Ⓤ Uhlandstrasse)

Eating

Kuchenladen CAFE €

7 ✕ MAP P108, B3

No one can resist the siren call of this classic cafe, whose homemade cakes are like works of art wrought from flour, sugar and cream. From cheesecake to carrot cake to the ridiculously rich Sachertorte, it's all

delicious down to the last crumb.
(☎030-3101 8424; www.derkuchen
laden.de; Kantstrasse 138; cakes €2.50-
4.50; ⏰10am-8pm Tue-Sun, noon-8pm
Mon; Ⓢ Savignyplatz)

Ali Baba ITALIAN €

8 🍴 MAP P108, C4

In business for more years
than there are robbers in the
eponymous fairy tale, Ali Baba is
a bustling port of call with local
cult status thanks to cheap and
simple but delicious thin-crust
pizzas, heaps of pasta and crusty
homemade bread for sopping up
the juices, all at bargain prices.
Separate vegan pizza menu.
(☎030-881 1350; www.alibaba-
berlin.de; Bleibtreustrasse 45; dishes
€4.50-15.50; ⏰noon-midnight; 🖋;
Ⓢ Savignyplatz)

Madame Ngo VIETNAMESE €€

9 🍴 MAP P108, B3

Set up in a former pharmacy,
Madame Ngo's *pho*-nomenal
soups may be just what the doctor ordered. Swimming in a rich
bone broth are tender chicken
bits, various cuts of beef or a
vegetable medley. Calling itself a
Hanoi-style brasserie, Madame's
also plays with French colonial
influences, such as pâté, *crevettes*
(shrimp) *de Paris* and fried quail.
(☎030-6027 4585; http://madame-
ngo.de; Kantstrasse 30; mains €9-17;
⏰noon-10pm)

Café-Restaurant Wintergarten im Literaturhaus INTERNATIONAL €€

10 🍴 MAP P108, D5

The hustle and bustle of Ku'damm
is only a block away from this
genteel late-19th-century villa
with attached literary salon and
bookshop. Tuck into dreamy cakes
or seasonal bistro cuisine amid
Old Berlin decor in the gracefully
stucco-ornamented rooms or, if
weather permits, in the idyllic garden. Breakfast is served until 2pm.
(☎030-882 5414; http://cafe-im-
literaturhaus.de; Fasanenstrasse 23;
mains €8-16; ⏰9am-midnight; 🖋;
Ⓤ Uhlandstrasse)

Berlin's Little Asia

It's not quite Chinatown,
but if you're in the mood for
the flavours of Asia, head to
Kantstrasse between Savi-
gnyplatz and Wilmersdorfer
Strasse. The strip is chock-a-
block with the city's densest
concentration of authentic
Chinese, Vietnamese and
Thai restaurants, including
the perennially popular Good
Friends (p114). At lunchtime
most offer value-priced specials, perfect for filling up on
the cheap.

Elevated Fast Food at Kantini

Kantini (Map p108, G3; www.bikiniberlin.de/de/kantini_und_restaurant; Bikini Berlin, Budapester Strasse; dishes €4-26; ⏰10am-8pm Mon-Sat; 🍴🚼; Ⓤ Zoologischer Garten, Ⓢ Zoologischer Garten) is a next-gen food court at the stylish Bikini Berlin shopping mall. It sports Instaworthy looks thanks to its mash-up of industrial edge and playful design touches, including potted plants, candy-coloured furniture and Zoo Berlin views. The 14 outlets pick up on international food trends – ramen and bibimbap to poke bowls – often with high quality.

Dicke Wirtin
GERMAN €€

11 ⊗ MAP P108, C3

Old Berlin charm is in every nook and cranny of this been-here-forever pub, which pours eight draught beers (including the superb Kloster Andechs) and nearly three dozen homemade schnapps varieties. Hearty local and German fare, such as meatballs in caper sauce, beef liver and pork roast, keeps brains balanced. Bargain lunches, too. (☎030-312 4952; www.dicke-wirtin.de; Carmerstrasse 9; mains €11-20; ⏰11am-late; Ⓢ Savignyplatz)

Good Friends
CHINESE €€

12 ⊗ MAP P108, B3

Good Friends is widely considered to be Berlin's best Cantonese restaurant. The ducks dangling in the window are merely an overture to a menu long enough to confuse Confucius, including plenty of authentic home-style dishes (on a separate menu). If steamed chicken feet prove too challenging, you can always fall back on sweet-and-sour pork or fried rice with shrimp. (☎030-313 2659; www.goodfriends-berlin.de; Kantstrasse 30; 2-course weekday lunch €7-7.70, dinner mains €11-20; ⏰noon-11pm; Ⓢ Savignyplatz)

Neni
INTERNATIONAL €€

13 ⊗ MAP P108, G3

This bustling greenhouse-style dining hall at the **25hours Hotel Bikini Berlin** (www.25hours-hotels.com; d €110-250; 🅿⊕❄@🛜) presents a spirited menu of meant-to-be-shared dishes inspired by Mediterranean, Iranian and Austrian cuisines. Top billing goes to the homemade falafel, the Jerusalem platter, the pulled-beef sandwich and the *knafeh* (a spirit-soaked dessert). The 10th-floor views of the zoo and the rooftops are a bonus. (☎030-120 221 200; www.neniberlin.de; Budapester Strasse 40; mains €6-30; ⏰noon-11pm; 🛜🍴; 🚌100, 200, Ⓢ Zoologischer Garten, Ⓤ Zoologischer Garten)

Mine Restaurant

ITALIAN €€€

14 MAP P108, E5

Italian restaurants may be a dime a dozen, but Mine's style, menu and service blend together as perfectly as a Sicilian stew. Helmed by Mikhail Mnatsakanov, the son of a Russian TV celebrity chef, it presents feistily flavoured next-gen fare from around the Boot by riffing on traditional recipes in innovative ways. The wine list makes even demanding oenophiles swoon. (📞030-8892 6363; www.minerestaurant.de; Meinekestrasse 10; mains €21-29; ⏱5.30-10pm; Ⓤ Uhlandstrasse)

Drinking

Bar Zentral

COCKTAIL BAR

15 Ⓖ MAP P108, E3

'Disappear here', beckons a blue neon sign at this top libation station run by two local bar gurus. Heed the call at the long wooden bar to pick through the palette of expertly crafted classics and new-falutin potions. The decor is both elegant and understated, and there are terrace tables for raising a pinkie alfresco on balmy evenings. (📞030-3743 3079; www.barzentral.de; Lotte-Lenya-Bogen 551; ⏱5pm-late; Ⓢ Zoologischer Garten, Ⓤ Zoologischer Garten, Kurfürstendamm)

Bikini Berlin (p118)

MASSIMO TODARO/SHUTTERSTOCK ©

Schleusenkrug BEER GARDEN

16 🚇 MAP P108, G1

Sitting pretty at the edge of Tiergarten park, next to a canal lock, Schleusenkrug has a charming 1950s interior but truly rocks beergarden season. People from all walks of life hunker over big mugs and comfort food – from grilled sausages to *Flammkuchen* (Alsatian pizza) and weekly specials (mains €9 to €17). Breakfast is served until 2pm. (📞030-313 9909; www.schleusenkrug.de; Müller-Breslau-Strasse; 🕑noon-midnight Mon-Sat, from 11am Sun; Ⓢ Zoologischer Garten, Tiergarten, Ⓤ Zoologischer Garten)

Diener Tattersall PUB

17 🚇 MAP P108, C4

In business for over a century, this Old Berlin haunt was taken over by German heavyweight champion Franz Diener in the 1950s and became one of West Berlin's iconic artist pubs. From Billy Wilder to Harry Belafonte, they all came for beer and *Bulette* (meat patties) and left behind signed black-and-white photographs that grace Diener's walls to this day. (📞030-881 5329; www.diener-berlin.de; Grolmanstrasse 47; 🕑6pm-2am Mon-Sat; Ⓢ Savignyplatz)

Monkey Bar BAR

18 🚇 MAP P108, G3

On the 10th floor of the 25hours Hotel Bikini Berlin (p114), this mainstream-hip 'urban jungle' delivers fabulous views of the city and Zoo Berlin, while the menu gives prominent nods to rum-based concoctions (great mai tai!) and has an inspired line-up of mocktails. Come early for chilled sundowners on the terrace. Different DJs spin nightly Friday to Sunday, from 4pm. (📞030-120 221 210; www.monkeybarberlin.de; Budapester Strasse 40; 🕑noon-2am; 📶; Ⓢ Zoologischer Garten, Ⓤ Zoologischer Garten)

Bar am Steinplatz COCKTAIL BAR

19 🚇 MAP P108, D2

This liquid playground at the art-deco **Hotel am Steinplatz** (www.hotelsteinplatz.com; r €100-290; 🅿🕑❄@📶🐾) has made history several times, most recently as Germany's first alcohol-free hotel-based cocktail bar. Mix-meister Willi Bittorf combines nonalcoholic distillates with kombucha, rose water, syrups, herbs and juices to create guilt- and hangover-free libations. Handy and hygienic: the menu is printed on the tables. (📞030-554 4440; http://barsteinplatz.com; Steinplatz 4; 🕑4pm-late; Ⓤ Ernst-Reuter-Platz)

Entertainment

Bar Jeder Vernunft CABARET

20 ⭐ MAP P108, E6

Life's still a cabaret at this intimate 1912 mirrored art-nouveau tent theatre, one of Berlin's most beloved venues for sophisticated song-and-dance shows, comedy and *chansons* (songs). Sip a glass of bubbly while relaxing at a candlelit cafe table or in a curvy red-velvet booth bathed in flickering candlelight that's reflected in the mirrors. Many shows don't require German-language skills. (☏030-883 1582; www.bar-jeder-vernunft.de; Schaperstrasse 24; admission varies; Ⓤ Spichernstrasse)

Zoo Palast
CINEMA

21 ✪ MAP P108, F3

Old-school glamour meets state-of-the-art technology and comfort at this rejuvenated grand cinema, which screens mostly 2D and 3D blockbusters (dubbed into German) in seven fancily appointed theatres. Check out the cool 1950s foyer. International stars can often be seen sashaying down the red carpet during the **Berlinale film festival** (www.berlinale.de; ☉Feb). (☏01805-222 966; www.zoopalast. premiumkino.de; Hardenbergstrasse 29a; tickets €11-19; 🚌100, 200, Ⓢ Zoologischer Garten, Ⓤ Zoologischer Garten)

Deutsche Oper Berlin
OPERA

22 ✪ MAP P108, A1

Founded by Berlin burghers in 1912 as a counterpoint to the royal opera on Unter den Linden, the Deutsche Oper presents a classic 19th-century opera repertory from Verdi and Puccini to Wagner and Strauss, all sung in their original languages. For contemporary, experimental and cross-cultural productions, check out what's on at the Tischlerei, the opera's joinery turned studio space. (German Opera Berlin; ☏030-3438 4343; www.deutscheoperberlin.de; Bismarckstrasse 35; tickets €20-180; Ⓤ Deutsche Oper)

A-Trane
JAZZ

23 ✪ MAP P108, B3

Herbie Hancock and Diana Krall are among the many world-class musicians who have graced the stage of this intimate jazz club. Mostly, though, it's top emerging global talent bringing their A-game to the A-Trane. Entry is free on Monday, when pianist Andreas Schmidt and his band get everyone's toes tapping. Concerts start promptly at 8pm. A cafe provides pre-concert sustenance. (☏030-313 2550; www.a-trane.de; Bleibtreustrasse 1; tickets €10-20; ☉8-11pm or later; Ⓢ Savignyplatz)

Schaubühne
THEATRE

24 ✪ MAP P108, A5

In a converted 1920s expressionist cinema by Erich Mendelsohn, Schaubühne is a top German stage for experimental, contemporary theatre, usually with a critical and analytical look at current social and political issues. The ensemble is directed by Thomas Ostermeier and includes many top names from German film and TV. Some performances feature English or French subtitles. (☏030-890 023; www.schaubuehne.de; Kurfürstendamm 153; tickets €7-49; Ⓤ Adenauerplatz)

Shopping

KaDeWe
DEPARTMENT STORE

25 🔒 MAP P108, H5

Continental Europe's largest department store has been going strong since 1907 and boasts an assortment so vast that a pirate-style campaign is the best way to plunder its bounty. If pushed for time, at least hurry up to the updated 6th-floor gourmet food hall. (www.kadewe.de; Tauentzienstrasse 21-24; ⏰10am-8pm Mon-Thu & Sat, to 9pm Fri; Ⓤ Wittenbergplatz)

Shopping Primer

Kurfürstendamm and Tauentzienstrasse are chock-a-block with outlets of international chains flogging fashion and accessories. Further west on Ku'damm are the more high-end boutiques such as Hermès, Cartier and Bulgari. Kantstrasse is the go-to zone for home designs. Connecting side streets, such as Bleibtreustrasse and Schlüterstrasse, house upscale indie and designer boutiques, bookshops and galleries, while Bikini Berlin features cutting-edge concept and flagship stores.

Manufactum
HOMEWARES

26 🔒 MAP P108, C1

Long before sustainable became a buzzword, this shop (the brainchild of a German Green Party member) stocked traditionally made quality products from around the world, many of which have stood the test of time. Cool finds include hand-forged iron pans by Turk, lavender soap from a French monastery and fountain pens by Lamy. (☏030-2403 3844; www.manufactum.de; Hardenbergstrasse 4-5; ⏰10am-8pm Mon-Fri, to 6pm Sat; Ⓤ Ernst-Reuter-Platz)

Bikini Berlin
MALL

27 🔒 MAP P108, G3

Germany's first concept mall opened in 2014 in a smoothly rehabilitated 1950s architectural icon nicknamed 'Bikini' because of its design: 200m-long upper and lower sections separated by an open floor, now chastely covered by a glass facade. Inside are three floors of urban indie boutiques, short-lease pop-up 'boxes' for up-and-comers, and an international street-food court. (☏030-5549 6455; www.bikini berlin.de; Budapester Strasse 38-50; ⏰shops 10am-8pm Mon-Sat, bldg 9am-8pm Mon-Sat; 📶; 🚌100, 200, Ⓤ Zoologischer Garten, Ⓢ Zoologischer Garten)

KaDeWe

Stilwerk

HOMEWARES

28 🔒 MAP P108, D3

This four-storey temple of good taste will have devotees of the finer things itching to redecorate. Everything you could possibly want for home and hearth is here, from key rings to grand pianos to vintage lamps. It's all housed in a striking modern building anchored by an open atrium clad in natural stone, maple and glass. (📞030-315 150; www.stilwerk.de/berlin; Kantstrasse 17; ⏰10am-7pm Mon-Sat; Ⓢ Savignyplatz)

Käthe Wohlfahrt

ARTS & CRAFTS

29 🔒 MAP P108, E4

With its mind-boggling assortment of traditional German Yuletide decorations and ornaments, this shop lets you celebrate Christmas year-round. It's accessed via a ramp that spirals around an 8m-high ornament-laden Christmas tree. (📞0800 409 0150; www. kaethe-wohlfahrt.com; Kurfürsten-damm 225-226; ⏰11am-5pm Mon-Sat; Ⓤ Kurfürstendamm)

Worth a Trip 🔭
Explore Schloss Charlottenburg

Schloss Charlottenburg is an exquisite baroque palace and the best place in Berlin to soak up the one-time grandeur of the royal Hohenzollern clan that ruled Brandenburg and later Prussia from 1415 to 1918. A visit is especially pleasant in summer, when you can fold a stroll around the palace garden into a day of peeking at royal treasures and lavishly furnished period rooms reflecting centuries of royal tastes and lifestyles.

📞 030-320 910

www.spsg.de

Spandauer Damm 10-22

Day pass to all open bldgs adult/concession €17/13

🕑 hours vary by bldg

🚌 M45, 109, 309,
Ⓤ Richard-Wagner-Platz, Sophie-Charlotte-Platz

Altes Schloss

The central Old Palace is fronted by Andreas Schlüter's grand **equestrian statue of the Great Elector** (1699). Inside, the baroque living quarters of Friedrich I and Sophie-Charlotte are an extravaganza in stucco, brocade and overall opulence. Highlights include the **Oak Gallery**, the charming **Oval Hall** overlooking the park, Friedrich I's **bedroom** and the **Eosander Chapel** with its trompe l'oeil arches. The king's passion for precious china is reflected in the dazzling **Porcelain Cabinet**, which is smothered in nearly 3000 pieces of Chinese and Japanese blue ware.

Neuer Flügel

The palace's most beautiful rooms are in the **new wing** (adult/concession incl tour or audioguide €12/8; ⏱10am-5.30pm Tue-Sun Apr-Oct, to 4.30pm Nov-Mar) extension, commissioned by Frederick the Great and designed in 1746 by the period's star architect Georg Wenzeslaus von Knobelsdorff. The confection-like **White Hall** and the **Golden Gallery**, a rococo fantasy of mirrors and gilding, are both standouts. Upstairs exhibits zero in on different facets of the king's personality and life at court. Also on view is a prized collection of **paintings** by Watteau, Pesne and other French 18th-century masters. Frederick the Great's nephew and successor added a summer residence with Chinese and Etruscan design elements as well as the more sombre **Winter Chambers**, where a bedroom designed by Schinkel for Queen Luise is standout.

Schlossgarten

The expansive palace park is part formal French, part unruly English and all picturesque playground. Hidden among the shady paths, flower beds, lawns, mature trees and carp pond are two smaller royal buildings: the sombre **Mausoleum** and the dainty **Belvedere**.

★ Top Tips

o Sold online, the 'Charlottenburg+' ticket (adult/concession €17/13) is a day pass valid for one-day admission to every open building.

o Avoid weekends, especially in summer.

o A palace visit is easily combined with a spin around the trio of adjacent art museums.

✖ Take a Break

o Enjoy a hearty German meal and a cold beer at **Brauhaus Lemke** (☎030-3087 8979; www.lemke.berlin; Luisenplatz 1; mains €7-15; ⏱5-9.30pm Mon & Tue, 1-9.30pm Wed-Fri, noon-9.30pm Sat & Sun), a short walk from the palace.

★ Getting There

Schloss Charlottenburg is 3km north-west of Zoologischer Garten.

U U7 to Richard-Wagner-Platz or U2 to Sophie-Charlotte-Platz, then 1km walk.

M45, 109 or 309 to Schloss Charlottenburg stop.

Worth a Trip Explore Schloss Charlottenburg

Neuer Pavillon

This Karl Friedrich Schinkel–designed **mini-palace** (adult/concession €4/3; 10am-5.30pm Tue-Sun Apr-Oct, noon-4pm Tue-Sun Nov-Mar) was a summer retreat modelled on neoclassical Italian villas. Today, it presents **paintings and sculpture** from the Biedermeier and romantic periods.

Mausoleum

The 1810 temple-shaped **Mausoleum** (adult/concession €3/2; 10am-5.30pm Tue-Sun Apr-Oct) was conceived as the final resting place of Queen Luise, and was twice expanded to make room for other royals. Their **marble sarcophagi** are exquisitely sculpted works of art.

Belvedere

The late-rococo Belvedere palace, with its distinctive cupola, got its start in 1788 as a private sanctuary for Friedrich Wilhelm II. It houses a precious porcelain collection and was expected to reopen at the end of 2021.

Nearby: Museum Berggruen

Picasso is especially well represented with paintings, drawings and sculptures from all major creative phases at this delightful **art museum** (030-266 424 242; www.smb.museum/mb; Schlossstrasse 1; adult/concession incl Sammlung Scharf-Gerstenberg €12/6; 10am-6pm Tue-Fri, from 11am Sat & Sun; P). Elsewhere it's off to Paul Klee's emotional world, Matisse's paper cut-outs, Giacometti's famous sculptures and a sprinkling of African art that inspired them all.

Nearby: Sammlung Scharf-Gerstenberg

This stellar **collection** (Schlossstrasse 70; adult/concession incl Museum Berggruen €12/6; 10am-6pm Tue-Fri, from 11am Sat & Sun) showcases 250 years of surrealist art, including works by René Magritte and Max Ernst. Standouts among their 18th-century forerunners include Goya's spooky etchings and the creepy dungeon scenes by Italian engraver Giovanni Battista Piranesi. Post-WWII surrealist interpretations are represented by Jean Dubuffet.

Nearby: Bröhan Museum

The **Bröhan Museum** (030-3269 0600; www.broehan-museum.de; Schlossstrasse 1a; adult/concession/child under 18yr €8/5/free; 10am-6pm Tue-Sun) trains the spotlight on art nouveau, art deco and functionalism furniture and design that rocked the aesthetics from the late 19th century until the 1930s. Its permanent exhibit displays covetable chairs, tables, teapots and other objects by such key protagonists as Hector Guimard, Peter Behrens, Josef Hoffmann and Wilhelm Wagenfeld.

SCHLOSS CHARLOTTENBURG

Ⓝ 0 ——————— 200 m
    0 ——————— 0.1 miles

Olbersstr

Brahestr

Tegeler Weg

Kamminer Str

Osnabrücker Str

Belvedere

Schlossgarten
Charlottenburg

Spree River

Karpfen-
teich

Mausoleum

Schlossgarten

Neuer
Pavillon

Tour Boat Landing
Schlossbrücke
Charlottenburg

Altes
Schloss

Neuer Flügel

Schloss
Charlottenburg

Brauhaus
Lemke

Spandauer Damm

Museum
Berggruen

Schlossstr

Sammlung
Scharf-
Gerstenberg

Bröhan
Museum

Walking Tour 🥾

A Saunter Through Schöneberg

Schöneberg flaunts a mellow middle-class identity but has a radical pedigree rooted in the '80s. Its multifaceted character nicely unfolds as you stroll from bourgeois Viktoria-Luise-Platz through Berlin's original gay quarter and along streets packed tight with boho cafes and smartly curated indie boutiques, to wind up at bustling Hauptstrasse where David Bowie bunked back in the '70s.

Getting There

Schöneberg sits between Kurfürstendamm and Kreuzberg.

Ⓤ This itinerary is bookended by two stations: Viktoria-Luise-Platz (U4) and Kleistpark (U7).

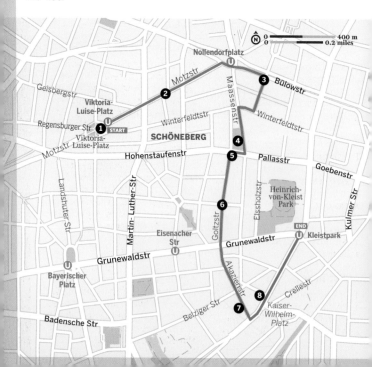

❶ Viktoria-Luise-Platz

Schöneberg's prettiest square is a classic baroque-style symphony of flower beds, big old trees, a lusty fountain and benches where locals swap gossip. It's framed by inviting cafes and 19th-century townhouses; note the ornate facades at Nos 7, 12 and 12a.

❷ Nollendorfplatz & the 'Gay Village'

Nollendorfplatz has been the gateway to Berlin's historic gay quarter since the 1920s, when Christopher Isherwood penned *Berlin Stories* (which inspired *Cabaret*) while living at Nollendorfstrasse 17. Rainbow flags still fly proudly above bars and businesses, especially along Motzstrasse and Fuggerstrasse. A memorial plaque at the U-Bahn station commemorates Nazi-era LGBTIQ+ victims.

❸ Street Art Museum

The **Urban Nation Museum** (www.urban-nation.com; Bülowstrasse 7; admission free; ⏱10am-6pm Tue & Wed, noon-8pm Thu-Sun) is a showcase of works by top urban artists. It pulls the genre out from the underpasses and abandoned buildings and makes it accessible to a wider audience.

❹ Farmers Market

If it's Wednesday or Saturday morning, you're in luck because ho-hum Winterfeldtplatz erupts with farm-fresh fare. Along with seasonal produce you'll find handmade cheeses, cured meats, olives, local honey and plenty more staples and surprises. Saturday also has artsy-craftsy stalls.

❺ Chocophile Alert

Winterfeldt Schokoladen
(☎030-2362 3256; www.winterfeldt-schokoladen.de; Goltzstrasse 23; ⏱10am-7pm Mon-Fri, to 6pm Sat, noon-6pm Sun) stocks a vast range of international handmade gourmet chocolates, all displayed gallery-style in the original oak fixtures of a 19th-century pharmacy that doubles as a cafe.

❻ Boutique-Hopping

Goltzstrasse and its extension Akazienstrasse teem with indie boutiques selling vintage threads, slinky underwear, handmade jewellery, exotic teas and cooking supplies. No high-street chain in sight.

❼ Double Eye

Javaholics cherish the award-winning espresso of **Double Eye** (☎0179 456 6960; Akazienstrasse 22; ⏱8.30am-6.30pm Mon-Fri, 9am-6.30pm Sat), which is why no one minds the inevitable queue.

❽ Hauptstrasse

The Turkish supermarket **Öz-Gida** (☎030-7871 5291; www.ozgida.de; Hauptstrasse 16; ⏱8am-8pm Mon-Sat) is known citywide for its olive selection, cheese spreads and quality meats. David Bowie and Iggy Pop shared a pad at Hauptstrasse 155.

Explore
Kreuzberg & Neukölln

Eastern Kreuzberg and northern Neukölln across the Landwehrkanal are the epicentres of freewheeling, multicultural and alternative Berlin and an energising combo of urban grit and hipster haven. Come here to track down fabulous street art, scarf a doner kebab, browse vintage stores and hang by the canal, then find out why the area is also known as the ultimate night-crawler's paradise.

The Short List

○ **Türkischer Markt (p140)** Immersing yourself in multicultural bounty on a crawl through the canal-side Turkish-German market.

○ **Kotti Bar-Hop (p128)** Soaking up the punky-funky alt-feel of eastern Kreuzberg.

○ **Badeschiff (p134)** Cooling down on a hot summer day in an old barge turned urban swimming pool.

○ **Klunkerkranich (p131)** Winding down a summer day parked under a sun sail at this cool rooftop bar.

○ **Street Food Thursday (p136)** Eating your way around the world at the weekly street-food party.

Getting There & Around

🚌 M29 links Potsdamer Platz with Oranienstrasse via Checkpoint Charlie; the M41 travels from Hauptbahnhof via Potsdamer Platz to Neukölln via Hermannplatz.

Ⓤ Kottbusser Tor (U8) puts you into the thick of things. For Neukölln, Schönleinstrasse, Hermannplatz and Boddinstrasse (all on the U8) as well as Rathaus Neukölln (U7) are key stops.

Neighbourhood Map on p132

Mural in Kreuzberg CAROL.ANNE/SHUTTERSTOCK ©

Walking Tour 🚶

Kotti Bar-Hop

Noisy, chaotic and sleepless, the area around Kottbusser Tor U-Bahn station (Kotti, for short) defiantly retains the alt-punky feel that's defined it since the 1970s. More gritty than pretty, this bee-hive of snack shops, cafes, pubs and bars delivers high-octane night-time action and is tailor-made for bar-hopping.

Walk Facts

Start Kottbusser Tor;
Ⓤ Kottbusser Tor

End Oranienstrasse;
Ⓤ Kottbusser Tor

Length 1.5km; one to six hours

❶ Funky Saloon

Tucked behind a pile of Turkish kebab shops, grocers and shisha bars, **Möbel Olfe** (☏030-2327 4690; www.moebel-olfe.de; Reichenberger Strasse 177; ⏰6-11pm Tue-Sun) is a queer-leaning drinking saloon that channels the area's alternative vibe with boho decor, strong Polish beers and a chatty ambience.

❷ Grape Delights

Great for earlier in the evening, **Otto Rink** (☏0163 706 8369; www. ottorink.de; Dresdener Strasse 124; ⏰6pm-2am) is an easy-going place to discover just how wonderful German wines can be. After 5pm on Sunday left-over glasses from opened bottles cost a mere €4.

❸ 1950s Cocktail Cave

If it's transcendent cocktails you're lusting after, point the compass to **Würgeengel** (☏030-615 5560; www.wuergeengel.de; Dresdener Strasse 122; ⏰from 7pm), a stylish art-deco-style bar with chandeliers and shiny black surfaces. The name pays homage to the surreal 1962 Buñuel movie *Exterminating Angel*.

❹ Luscious Lair

A fixture on Kreuzberg's hipster circuit, the vintage decor at **Luzia** (www.facebook.com/luziabar; Oranienstrasse 34; ⏰from noon Tue-Sun) gets updated with a mural by street artist Chin Chin. It's a comfy spot with lighting that gives even pasty-faced hipsters a glow.

❺ Gateway to Hell

The **Trinkteufel** (Drink Devil; ☏030-614 7128; www.facebook.com/ TrinkteufelKreuzberg; Naunynstrasse 60; ⏰from 2pm) punk pub ('Drink Devil', subtitled 'gateway to hell') is the dive bar where Pete Doherty downed a few before smashing a car window and getting briefly arrested. Regulars couldn't care less as long as the beer is cheap and the music loud.

❻ Easy Medicine

Whatever ails you may well be fixed after dropping by the **Apotheken Bar** (☏030-6951 8108; www.facebook. com/apothekenbar; Mariannenplatz 6; ⏰5-11pm Tue-Sat), a vintage-styled outpost in a 19th-century pharmacy. The original fixtures and old objects like a scale, bottles and signs form the atmospheric setting for expert cocktails, some featuring homemade tonic water and other potions.

❼ Camp of Glam

A mash-up of trash, camp and fun, **Roses** (☏030-615 6570; Oranienstrasse 187; ⏰10pm-6am) is a beloved pit stop for queers and their friends. Don't let the furry walls and a predominance of the colour pink distract you from the fact that this place takes drinking seriously until the early morning hours.

Walking Tour 🚶

Nosing Around Neukölln

Northern Neukölln knows what it's like to go from troubled neighbourhood to hipster haven. For decades the area made headlines, mostly for its high crime rate and poor schools, only to get 'discovered' a few years ago by a cash-poor and idea-rich international crowd. Today the 'hood flaunts a thriving DIY ethos and teems with funky bars, galleries, project spaces and cafes, many of them run by creative expats.

Walk Facts

Start Maybachufer; Ⓤ Schönleinstrasse

End Neukölln Arcaden; Ⓤ Rathaus Neukölln

Length 3km; one to two hours without stops

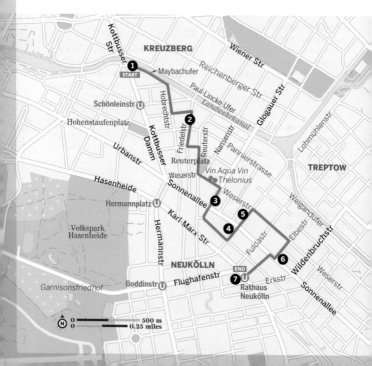

❶ Canalside Marketeering

Start by walking along the Maybachufer, a scenic section of the Landwehrkanal, ideally on Tuesday or Friday afternoons when the Türkischer Markt (p140) is in full swing. Join hipsters in their quest for exotic cheese spreads, crusty flatbreads and mountains of produce.

❷ Frosty Delights

Ice-cream parlour **Fräulein Frost** (☎030-9559 5521; www.fräulein-frost.de; Friedelstrasse 38; per scoop €1.40-1.70; ⏰noon-6pm or later; 🐾) is all about experimentation, as reflected in such courageous – and delectable – concoctions as apple-ginger or GuZiMi, which stands for Gurke-Zitrone-Minze (cucumber-lemon-mint).

❸ Burger Bonanza

The folks at **Berlin Burger International** (☎0160 482 6505; www.berlinburgerinternational.com; Pannierstrasse 5; burgers €8-10.70; ⏰noon-10pm Mon-Wed, to 11pm Thu-Sun; 🐾) know that size matters. At least when it comes to burgers: handmade, two-fisted, bulging and sloppy contenders.

❹ 'Arab' Street

Usually busy as a beehive, **Azzam** (☎030-6097 7541; Sonnenallee 54; mains €4-6; ⏰8am-1am; 🚌M41) transplants Beirut's palpable energy to bustling Sonnenallee (nicknamed 'Arab Street'). Try its heavenly hummus, crispy falafel or crunchy *fatteh* (an addictive mash-up of fried pita bits, cashews and chickpeas drizzled with yoghurt) to see what the fuss is all about.

❺ Sustainable Chic

At **Shio Store** (www.shiostore.com; Weichselstrasse 59; ⏰noon-7pm), Kate Pinkstone tailors chic, timeless and sustainable pieces from linen, organic cotton jersey and upcycled cotton in her studio located right behind the elegantly minimalist store.

❻ Divine Baklava

Damaskus Konditorei (☎030-7037 0711; www.damaskus-konditorei-emissa.com; Sonnenallee 93; snacks from €2; ⏰9am-10pm Mon-Sat, noon-8pm Sun) stands out for its truly artistic and rave-worthy pastries. Try its rich *kanafeh* (cheese-filled pastry drenched in syrup) or signature *halawat al jubn* (rosewater cheese pockets).

❼ Rooftop Chilling

The Insta-perfect views are only the overture of **Klunkerkranich** (www.klunkerkranich.org; Karl-Marx-Strasse 66; €3-6, before 4pm free; ⏰4pm-2am, open earlier summer; 📶), a constantly evolving and always packed cafe-bar-club-garden-culture-venue in the sky. Find it on the top parking deck of the Neukölln Arcaden shopping mall.

A B C D

1

Oranienstr

Heinrich-Heine-Str

Heinrich-Heine-Platz

Engeldamm

Bethaniendamm

Wrangelstr

Mariannenplatz

★ 24

27 🚇

Muskauer Str

Dresdener Str

Leuschnerdamm

Waldemarstr

Ritterstr

Rifferstr

✕ 12

Oranienplatz

✕ 9

Prinzenstr

Rifferstr

Reichenberger Str

Dresdener Str

✕ 10

Adalbertstr

🚇 28

Oranienstr

Naunynstr

Heinrichplatz

Muskauer Str

Manteuffelstr

Görlitzer Bahnhof

2

Prinzenstr 🚇

Wassertorplatz

Astronaut Mural

🔒 25

Nature Morte

Prinzenstr

Gitschiner Str

🚇

Kottbusser Tor

Kottbusser Str

Skalitzer Str

KREUZBERG

Böckler Park

Urbanhafen

Admiralstr

Fraenkelufer

Planufer

Marianenstr

🔒 30

19

🔒

26

Paul-Lincke-Ufer

Maybachufer

Landwehrkanal

Manteuffelstr

Reichenberger Str

Lausitzer Str

3

Urbanstr

Grimmstr

Böckhstr

Dieffenbachstr

Kottbusser Damm

✕ 7

Bürknerstr

Schönleinstr 🚇

Sanderstr

🔒 29

Friedelstr

4

Körtestr

Fichtestr

Graefestr

Hohenstaufenplatz

Urbanstr

Pflügerstr

Kottbusser Damm

17 🔒

NEUKÖLLN

Hobrechtstr

15 🍷

Reuterstr

Reuterplatz

✕ 13

✕ 8

Südstern 🚇

★ 23

Hasenheide

Cemeteries

6

✕

★ 3

Hasenheide

Hermannplatz

Hermannplatz 🚇

Sonnenallee

Hermannstr

Karl-Marx-Str

5

6

For reviews see

◉ Sights   p134
✕ Eating   p134
🍷 Drinking   p138
★ Entertainment   p139
🔒 Shopping   p140

Volkspark Hasenheide

Ⓝ 0   400 m
0   0.2 miles

Sights

Badeschiff SWIMMING

1 MAP P132, H3

Take an old river barge, fill it with water, moor it in the Spree and – voila! – you get an artist-designed urban lifestyle pool that's a popular swim-and-chill spot. With music blaring, a sandy beach, wooden decks, lots of hot bods and a bar to fuel the fun, the vibe is distinctly 'Ibiza on the Spree'. (☑0162 545 1374; www.arena-berlin.de; Eichenstrasse 4; adult/concession €6.50/3.50; ⏱from 8am May–Sep; 🚌265, 🚆Treptower Park, Ⓤ Schlesisches Tor)

Eating

Café Mugrabi ISRAELI €

2 🍴 MAP P132, F3

Feel-good Café Mugrabi ticks all the boxes of meatless Levantine classics, including finger-lickin' hummus, tangy shakshuka and roasted cauliflower. It's often filled to the hilt, but the team remains remarkably chill under pressure. In summer, grab a table with a view of Görlitzer Park. Most dishes can be made vegan. (☑030-2658 5400; www.cafemugrabi.com; Görlitzer Strasse 58; mains €6.50-13; ⏱11am-9pm Wed-Mon; 🥗; Ⓤ Görlitzer Bahnhof)

Con Tho VIETNAMESE €

3 🍴 MAP P132, C5

Punctuated by bamboo and paper lanterns, Con Tho ('rabbit' in Vietnamese) is a feel-good vegan-vegetarian burrow that gives traditional recipes a contempo workout. Dip into a pool of mouth-watering goodness with the 'happy to share' small plates, or pick your favourite rice bowl, stuffed rice-flour crêpe or lemongrass-annatto-based soup. (☑030-2245 6122; http://con-tho-restaurant.de; Hasenheide 16; dishes €3.50-9; ⏱noon-midnight; 🥗; Ⓤ Hermannplatz)

Sironi BAKERY €

4 🍴 MAP P132, E2

The focaccia and ciabatta are as good as they get without taking a flight to Italy, thanks to Alfredo Sironi, who hails from the Boot and now treats Berlin breadlovers to his habit-forming carb creations. Watch the flour magicians whip up the next batch in his glass bakery right in the iconic **Markthalle Neun** (☑030-6107 3473; www.markthalleneun.de; ⏱noon-6pm Mon-Wed & Fri, noon-10pm Thu, 10am-6pm Sat), then order a piece to go. (www.facebook.com/sironi.de; Markthalle Neun, Eisenbahnstrasse 42; snacks from €2.50; ⏱8am-8pm Mon-Wed, Fri & Sat, to 10pm Thu; Ⓤ Görlitzer Bahnhof)

Burgermeister BURGERS €

5 🍴 MAP P132, F2

It's green, ornate, a century old and...it used to be a toilet. Fast forward to 2006, when the original branch of this fast-growing Berlin burger franchise opened in this unlikely location beneath the elevated U-Bahn tracks. There's always a wait for the plump all-beef patties

Top Five Kreuzberg Murals

Berlin has emerged as Europe's street-art capital, with some major local and international talent havin left their mark on the city. Check out these five landmark murals.

Astronaut/Kosmonaut (Map p132, C2; Marianenstrasse; U Kottbusser Tor) Victor Ash's monumental stencil-style piece was inspired by the US–Soviet space race.

Pink Man (Map p132, G2; Falckensteinstrasse 48; U Schlesisches Tor) House-sized mural by Blu depicts a creature composed of hundreds of writhing pink bodies, plus a lone white guy crouched on its finger.

Rounded Heads (Map p132, F2; Oppelner Strasse 46-47; U Schlesisches Tor) Internationally renowned Berlin street artist Nomad created this faceless person embracing a hooded character.

Yellow Man (Map p132, F2; Oppelner Strasse 3; U Schlesisches Tor) This bizarrely dressed, seemingly genderless, yellow-skinned figure is a signature work by Brazilian twins Os Gemeos.

Nature Morte (Map p132, D2; cnr Oranienstrasse & Manteuffelstrasse; U Görlitzer Bahnhof) With his animal carcasses, Belgian artist ROA illustrates the cycle of life and death in a distinctive monochrome spray-paint style.

tucked between a brioche bun – but it's so worth it! (☎030-403 645 320; www.burger-meister.de; Oberbaumstrasse 8; burgers €3.50-7; ⊗11am-1am Mon-Wed, 11am-2am Thu-Sat, noon-midnight Sun; U Schlesisches Tor)

Masaniello ITALIAN €

6 ⊗ MAP P132, C5

The tables are almost too small for the wagon-wheel-size certified-Neapolitan pizzas tickled by wood fire at Luigi and Pascale's old-school pizza institution. On Friday and Saturday the pies get competition from the grilled fresh-fish platters that are perfect for sharing with your posse. On balmy summer nights, the spacious, flowery terrace practically transports you to Italy. (☎030-692 6657; www.masaniello.de; Hasenheide 20; pizza €8-11.50; ⊗noon-11pm Wed-Mon; U Hermannplatz)

Cafe Jacques MEDITERRANEAN €€

7 ⊗ MAP P132, D4

Like a fine wine, this French-Mediterranean darling keeps improving with age. Candlelit wooden tables and art-festooned brick walls feel as welcoming as an old

Street Food Thursday

🍽️

Every Thursday evening since 2013, this Berlin institution sees a couple of dozen or so aspiring chefs set up their food stalls in **Markthalle Neun** (www.markthalleneun.de; Eisenbahnstrasse 42-43; ⏰5-10pm Thu; Ⓤ Görlitzer Bahnhof), a historic market hall in Kreuzberg, and serve up delicious global street food. Order your favourites, lug them to a communal table and gobble them up with a glass of Heidenpeters, a craft beer brewed right on the premises.

friend's embrace. Owner Ahmad is an impeccable host who'll happily advise you on the perfect wine to match to your blackboard-menu pick. Expect a rotating festival of tantalising dishes, often with unexpected flavour combinations. Cash only. (📞030-694 1048; http://cafejacques.de; Maybachufer 14; mains €12.50-19.50; ⏰noon-10pm; Ⓤ Schönleinstrasse)

Fes Turkish BBQ   TURKISH €€

8 🍴 MAP P132, A5

If you like a communal DIY approach to dining, gather your friends for a grill-fest at this contemporary Turkish restaurant. Give strips of marinated chicken, beef fillet and tender lamb the perfect tan on the electric grill sunk right into your rustic wooden table while you spread a rainbow of homemade

meze onto the freshly baked bread – pure bliss! (📞030-2391 7778; http://fes-turkishbbq.de; Hasenheide 58; meze €4-11, meat from €16; ⏰5-11pm Tue-Sun; Ⓤ Südstern)

Orania. Restaurant   INTERNATIONAL €€

9 🍴 MAP P132, B2

Punctilious artisanship meets boundless creativity at cosmo-chic Orania.Restaurant, where a small army of chefs fusses around culinary wunderkind Philipp Vogel in the shiny open kitchen. Only three ingredients find their destiny in each dish, inspired by global flavours rather than food fads. Must try: Vogel's magic 'Xberg Duck', which deconstructs the bird into four delectable courses (€54, two-person minimum). (📞030-6953 9680; https://orania.berlin/restaurant; Oranienstrasse 40; dishes €16-20; ⏰lunch noon-3pm, dinner 6-10pm; Ⓤ Moritzplatz)

Ora   EUROPEAN €€

10 🍴 MAP P132, B2

A 19th-century pharmacy has been splendidly rebooted as a stylishly casual wine restaurant. The antique wooden medicine cabinets are now the back bar, where craft beer and cocktails are dispensed to those with an appreciation for the finer things in life. The daily calibrated modern brasserie menu is a composition of whatever trusted regional suppliers deliver that morning. (📞030-5486 1070; http://ora.berlin; Oranienplatz 14;

2-/3-/4-course dinner €35/42/49, lunch incl 1 glass wine €19; ⏱5.30pm-midnight Wed, 12.30pm-midnight Thu-Sat, 4-11pm Sun; Ⓤ Kottbusser Tor)

Freischwimmer INTERNATIONAL €€

11 ⓧ MAP P132, H3

In fine weather, few places are more idyllic than this rustic 1930s boathouse turned canal-side chill zone. The menu runs from meat and fish cooked on a lava-rock grill to crisp salads, *Flammkuchen* (Alsatian pizza) and seasonal specials. It's also a popular Sunday brunch spot. (☎030-6107 4309; www.freischwimmer-berlin.com; Vor dem Schlesischen Tor 2; mains brunch & lunch €8-12, dinner €10-22; ⏱noon-late Mon-Fri, from 10am Sat & Sun; 🛜; Ⓢ Treptower Park, Ⓤ Schlesisches Tor)

Max und Moritz GERMAN €€

12 ⓧ MAP P132, B1

The patina of yesteryear hangs over this ode-to-old-school gastropub, named for the cheeky Wilhelm Busch cartoon characters. Since 1902, it has packed hungry diners and thirsty drinkers into its rustic tile-and-stucco-ornamented rooms for sudsy home brews and granny-style Berlin fare. A menu favourite is the *Königsberger Klopse* (veal meatballs in caper sauce). (☎030-6951 5911; www.maxundmoritzberlin.de; Oranienstrasse 162; mains €9-20; ⏱5-11pm Wed-Mon; 🛜; Ⓤ Moritzplatz)

Tulus Lotrek INTERNATIONAL €€€

13 ⓧ MAP P132, B5

This next-gen Michelin-starred restaurant has all you could wish

Markthalle Neun

JJFARQ/SHUTTERSTOCK ©

for: fantastic food, to-die-for wines and conversation-sparking design, all wrapped into a feel-good vibe of disarming irreverence. Meisterchef Max Strohe fearlessly blends a global range of products into intensely aromatic and intellectually ambitious food with soul. The secret ingredient to Tulus Lotrek's success, though, is the forever-smiling Ilona Scholl, the quintessential host. (☎030-4195 6687; www.tuluslotrek.de; Fichtestrasse 24; 6-/8-course tasting menu €130/160; ☺6-11pm Thu-Mon; ♪; Ⓤ Südstern)

eins44 EUROPEAN €€€

14 ✖ MAP P132, F6

This casual fine-dining outpost in a late-19th-century distillery serves meals with robust flavours and a strong native identity, composed largely with seasonally hunted and gathered ingredients. Competing with the kitchen compositions is the lofty dining room's industrial charm, accented by black-and-white metro tiles, metal lamps and hefty beech-wood tables. (☎030-6298 1212; www.eins44.com; 3rd courtyard, Elbestrasse 28/29; mains €22-28; ☺5-10pm; 🛜; 🚌M41, 104, 166, Ⓤ Rathaus Neukölln)

Drinking

Truffle Pig COCKTAIL BAR

15 🍷 MAP P132, D5

No need to ferret through dirt, but a little intuition will help you find clandestine cocktail lair Truffle Pig. Hint: push the fire-alarm button at the back of the Kauz & Kiebitz

craft-beer pub to gain access to this complexion-friendly realm of elevated imbibing designed by the same studio as club legend Berghain. (☎0176 3433 8558; http://trufflepigberlin.de; Reuterstrasse 47; ☺8am-late Wed-Sat; 🚌M41, Ⓤ Hermannplatz, Schönleinstrasse)

Velvet Bar COCKTAIL BAR

16 🍷 MAP P132, E6

This first-rate drinking den is the perfect spot for an evening of paced imbibing. Boutique spirits, seasonal ingredients and unusual techniques (involving a centrifuge or an ultrasonic bath) conspire to create cocktails that are like alchemy in a glass.

No surprise that Velvet snagged Germany's 'Bar of the Year' title in 2019, just a year and a half after its opening. (www.velvet-bar-berlin.de; Ganghoferstrasse 1; ☺7pm-late Wed-Mon; Ⓤ Rathaus Neukölln)

Geist im Glass BAR

17 🍷 MAP P132, D4

Weekends wouldn't be the same without Aishah Bennett's soul-restoring brunches (buttermilk pancakes, Bloody Marys, bottomless filter coffee!). But, frankly, swinging by this cabin-style lair is a clever endeavour any night. Get comfortable with immaculate cocktails and well-curated craft-beer and wine selections. Quality is tops and prices fair. (☎0152 5135 3816; www.facebook.com/geistimglas; Lenaustrasse 27; ☺6-11pm Mon-Fri, 10am-3pm & 6-11pm Sat & Sun; Ⓤ Hermannplatz)

Birgit & Bier
BEER GARDEN

18 MAP P132, H3

Enter through the iron gate and embark on a magical mystery tour that'll have you chilling in the funky beer garden, taking selfies on a huge Hollywood swing, lounging in a retired carousel or dancing under the disco ball. (☎0162 694 1825; www.birgit.berlin; Schleusenufer 3; ⏰hours vary; ☐165, 265, N65, ⑤Treptower Park, ⓤSchlesisches Tor)

Ankerklause
PUB

19 MAP P132, C3

Ahoy there! Drop anchor at this nautical-kitsch tavern in an old harbour master's shack to give the classic jukebox a workout over cold beers and surprisingly good German pub fare. The best seats are on the Landwehrkanal-facing terrace, where you can wave at swans and boats puttering past. A cult pit stop from breakfast until the wee hours. (☎030-693 5649; www.ankerklause.de; Kottbusser Damm 104; ⏰4pm-late Mon, from 10am Tue-Sun; ⓤSchönleinstrasse)

Hopfenreich
PUB

20 MAP P132, F2

Since 2014, Berlin's first dedicated craft-beer bar has been plying punters with a changing roster of close to a couple of dozen global ales, IPAs and other brews on tap – both known and obscure. It's all served with street-cred flourish in a corner pub near the Schlesische Strasse party mile. (☎030-8806 1080; www.hopfenreich.de; Sorauer Strasse 31; ⏰from 4pm; ⓤSchlesisches Tor)

Entertainment

Comedy Café Berlin
COMEDY

21 MAP P132, F6

This vivacious bar offers stand-up and improv shows in English five nights a week, with many free shows and a lot of varied performances from Berlin's burgeoning English comedy scene. In addition to laughs, there are super-cheesy toasties, a great selection of spirits, and craft beer on tap. (CCB; www.comedycafeberlin.com; Roseggerstrasse 17; ⏰7-11pm Wed-Sun; ☐Geygerstrasse, ⓤKarl-Marx-Strasse)

Wolf Kino
CINEMA

22 MAP P132, F6

The antidote to binge-streaming is crowdfunded Wolf, a two-screen bastion of international indie cinema tucked into a former brothel. After taking in a quirky flick, pull up a chair in the attached cafe-bar for drinks and deep discussions with fellow cineasts. With any luck, you might even get to meet the film-maker(s). (☎030-921 039 333; www.wolfberlin.org; Weserstrasse 59; adult/concession €9/8; ☐M41, 104, 166, ⓤRathaus Neukölln)

English Theatre Berlin
THEATRE

23 MAP P132, A5

Berlin's oldest English-language theatre puts on an engaging roster of in-house productions, plays by international visiting troupes, concerts, comedy, dance and cabaret by local performers. Quality is often high and the cast international. Most tickets cost €16.50. (☎030-691 1211; www.etberlin.de; Fidicinstrasse 40; 🚌M19, Ⓤ Platz der Luftbrücke)

Freiluftkino Kreuzberg

OUTDOOR CINEMA

24 ⭐ MAP P132, C1

This beloved open-air cinema screens international current-season, classic and cult flicks in digital quality on the courtyard lawn behind the **Kunstquartier Bethanien** (www.kunstquartier-bethanien.de; Mariannenplatz 2; admission free; 🕙10am-8pm Sun-Wed, to 10pm Thu-Sat) arts centre. All movies are presented in the original language with German subtitles; German movies have English subtitles.

All screenings take place rain or shine. (☎030-2936 1628; www.freiluftkino-kreuzberg.de; Mariannenplatz; tickets €8.50; 🕙May-early Sep; Ⓤ Kottbusser Tor)

Shopping

UKO Fashion Berlin

FASHION & ACCESSORIES

25 🔒 MAP P132, C2

In her little shop, Doritt Körzell has shown a steady hand at making clued-up locals look good in fashionable yet affordable threads for over 20 years. Originally a secondhand store, her focus today is on new clothing and accessories from international labels that you wouldn't find in the high-street chains. (☎0177 691 8581; www.uko-fashion.de; Oranienstrasse 201; 🕙11am-8pm Mon-Fri, to 4pm Sat; Ⓤ Görlitzer Bahnhof)

Türkischer Markt

MARKET

26 🔒 MAP P132, C3

This bazaar-like market along the Landwehrkanal is sure to bring a gleam to foodies' eyes. Join global hipsters, pram-pushing parents and curious tourists for a bewildering bounty of seasonal fruit and veg, Middle Eastern specialities and everything from fabric to organic teas. Popularity has pushed up selection and quality along with prices, but late in the day bargains still abound. (Turkish Market; www.tuerkenmarkt.de; Maybachufer; 🕙11am-6.30pm Tue & Fri; Ⓤ Schönleinstrasse)

Folkdays

FASHION & ACCESSORIES

27 🔒 MAP P132, D1

The folks from Folkdays travel the world to build relationships with skilled artisans who produce contemporary fashion, accessories and homewares using time-tested techniques passed down through generations. Whether you fall in love with an alpaca sweater from Peru, handwoven baskets from Morocco or recycled brass earrings from Kenya, you can be sure it's fair trade at its finest. (☎030-9362 6094; www.folkdays.com; Manteuffelstrasse 19; 🕙noon-7pm Mon-Fri, to 6pm Sat; Ⓤ Görlitzer Bahnhof)

Türkischer Markt

VooStore

FASHION & ACCESSORIES

28 🔒 MAP P132, C2

Kreuzberg's first concept store presents its covetables in an old backyard locksmith shop off gritty Oranienstrasse. In suitably austere-chic surrounds, it stocks fashion-forward designer threads and accessories, along with cool books, gadgets, mags and spirits. The in-house Companion Cafe serves speciality coffees and tea from its own micro-farm. (📞030-6165 1112; www.vooberlin.com; Oranienstrasse 24; ⏱10am-8pm Mon-Sat; ⓤKottbusser Tor)

Nowkoelln Flowmarkt

MARKET

29 🔒 MAP P132, D4

This flea market sets up twice monthly along the scenic Maybachufer and delivers secondhand bargains galore, along with handmade threads and jewellery. (www. nowkoelln.de; Maybachufer; ⏱10am-5pm 2nd & 4th Sun of month Mar-Dec; ⓤKottbusser Tor, Schönleinstrasse)

Hard Wax

MUSIC

30 🔒 MAP P132, C3

This well-hidden record shop, in business since 1989, is a seminal stop for fans of electronic music in all its permutations. (📞030-6113 0111; www.hardwax.com; 3rd fl, door A, 2nd courtyard, Paul-Lincke-Ufer 44a; ⏱noon-8pm Mon-Sat; ⓤKottbusser Tor)

MATYAS REHAK/SHUTTERSTOCK ©

Walking Tour 🥾

An Afternoon in the Bergmannkiez

One of Berlin's most charismatic neighbourhoods, the Bergmannkiez in western Kreuzberg is named for its main shopping strip, the Bergmannstrasse, which is chock-a-block with cafes and indie shops. Above it all 'soars' the Kreuzberg hill, Berlin's highest natural elevation. If you've got time, be sure to make a detour to nearby Tempelhof Airport, which has been rebooted as a vast urban park.

Walk Facts

Start Marheineke Markthalle; Ⓤ Gneisenaustrasse (U7)

End Curry 36; Ⓤ Mehringdamm (U6, U7)

Length 3.5km; two to three hours

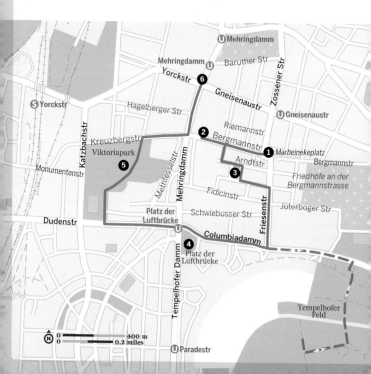

❶ Marheineke Markthalle

The aisles of the renovated 19th-century **Marheineke Markthalle** (www.meine-markthalle.de; Marheinekeplatz; 8am-8pm Mon-Fri, to 6pm Sat) brim with vendors plying everything from organic sausages to handmade cheeses, artisanal honey and other bounty.

❷ Picknweight Store

Vintage fans love this huge loft **store** (030-694 3348; https://picknweight.de; 1st fl, Bergmannstrasse 102; noon-7pm Mon-Thu, to 8pm Fri & Sat) crammed with used clothing going back to the 1960s, all priced by the kilo (€25 to €95). Enter via the courtyard.

❸ Chamissoplatz

With its ornate townhouses, cobbled streets, old-timey lanterns and octagonal pissoir, Chamissoplatz looks virtually unchanged since the late 19th century, making this square a popular film set.

❹ Luftbrückendenkmal

The **Berlin Airlift Memorial** (Berlin Airlift Memorial; Platz der Luftbrücke; P) outside the former Tempelhof Airport honours those who participated in keeping the city fed and free during the 1948–49 Berlin Blockade. The trio of spikes represents the three air corridors used by the Western Allies, while the plinth bears the names of the 79 people who died in this colossal effort.

❺ Viktoriapark

Take a break in this rambling park draped over the 66m-high Kreuzberg hill, home to a vineyard, a waterfall and a pompous memorial commemorating Napoleon's 1815 defeat. In summer, laid-back locals arrive to chill, tan or enjoy drinks at **Golgatha** (030-785 2453; www.golgatha-berlin.de; Dudenstrasse 48-64; 9am-late Apr-Sep;) beer garden.

❻ Curry 36

Day after day, night after night, a motley crowd – cops, cabbies, queens, office jockeys, savvy tourists etc – wait their turn at **Curry 36** (030-2580 088 336; www.curry36.de; Mehringdamm 36; snacks €2-6; 9am-11pm), a top *Currywurst* purveyor that's been frying 'em up since 1981.

✗ Optional Detour: Tempelhofer Feld

To extend your walk, swing by **Tempelhofer Feld** (www.gruen-berlin.de/tempelhofer-feld; admission free; sunrise-sunset;), a huge untamed urban park on the airfield of decommissioned Tempelhof Airport. Budget an hour or more to explore this noncommercial open-sky playground with a beer garden, an artsy minigolf course, barbecue areas and urban gardening.

Explore
Friedrichshain

The former East Berlin district of Friedrichshain is famous for such high-profile Cold War–era relics as the longest surviving stretch of Berlin Wall (the East Side Gallery), the socialist boulevard Karl-Marx-Allee and the former Stasi headquarters. But the area also stakes it reputation on having Berlin's most rambunctious nightlife scene, with a glut of clubs and bars to get your groove on.

The Short List

○ **East Side Gallery (p146)** *Checking out the street art festooning a 1.3km-long vestige of the Berlin Wall.*

○ **RAW Gelände (p156)** *Partying till sunrise and beyond in the rough-around-the-edges venues at this former train-repair station.*

○ **Flea market (p157)** *Foraging for treasure at this Sunday sell-a-thon on Boxhagener Platz.*

○ **Karl-Marx-Allee (p150)** *Marvelling at the monumental socialist architecture flanking this Cold War–era boulevard.*

Getting There & Around

⑤ Ostbahnhof and Warschauer Strasse are handy for the East Side Gallery; Warschauer Strasse and Ostkreuz for Boxhagener Platz and Revaler Strasse.

Ⓤ U1 goes west from Warschauer Strasse via Kreuzberg and Schöneberg to Charlottenburg; the U5 links with Hauptbahnhof.

🚊 M10 and M13 link Warschauer Strasse with Prenzlauer Berg.

Neighbourhood Map on p148

Karl-Marx-Allee (p150) STAVROS ARGYROPOULOS/SHUTTERSTOCK ©

Top Experience 📷

Walk Along the East Side Gallery

In 1989, after 28 years, the Berlin Wall, that grim divider of humanity, was finally torn down. Most of it was quickly dismantled, but along Mühlen- strasse, a 1.3km stretch became the East Side Gallery, the world's largest open-air mural strip. Today it's a memorial to the fall of the Wall and the peaceful reunification that followed.

◉ MAP P148, B5

www.eastsidegallery berlin.de

tours adult/concession €3.50/2.50

U Warschauer Strasse,
S Ostbahnhof, War- schauer Strasse

Dmitri Vrubel: My God, Help Me to Survive This Deadly Love

The gallery's best-known painting – showing Soviet and GDR leaders Leonid Brezhnev and Erich Honecker locking lips with eyes closed (pictured) – is based on an actual photograph taken by French journalist Remy Bossu during Brezhnev's 1979 Berlin visit. This kind of fraternal kiss was an expression of great respect in socialist countries.

Birgit Kinder: Test the Rest

Another favourite is Kinder's painting of a GDR-era Trabant car bursting through the Wall with the licence plate reading 'November 9, 1989'. Originally called Test the Best, the artist renamed her work after the image's 2009 restoration.

Kani Alavi: It Happened in November

A wave of people being squeezed through a breached Wall in a metaphorical rebirth reflects Alavi's recollection of the events of 9 November 1989. Note the different expressions on the faces, ranging from hope, joy and euphoria to disbelief and fear.

Thierry Noir: Homage to the Young

This Berlin-based French artist has done work for Wim Wenders and U2, but he's most famous for these cartoon-like heads. Naive, simple and boldly coloured, they symbolise the new-found freedom that followed the Wall's collapse. Noir was one of the few artists who had painted the western side of the Wall before its demise.

Thomas Klingenstein: Detour to the Japanese Sector

Born in East Berlin, Klingenstein spent time in a Stasi prison for dissent before being extradited to West Germany in 1980. This mural was inspired by his childhood love for Japan, where he ended up living from 1984 to the mid-'90s.

★ Top Tips

o The more famous paintings are near the Ostbahnhof end, so start your walk here if you've got limited time.

o For more street art and graffiti, check out the river-facing side of the East Side Gallery.

o The grassy strip between the gallery and Spree River is a nice spot for chilling with a picnic or a cold beer. There are supermarkets in the Ostbahnhof.

✕ Take a Break

o The Floating Lounge bar at the **Eastern Comfort Hostelboat** (☎030-6676 3806; www.eastern-comfort.com; Mühlenstrasse 73; dm/d from €16/58; ⊗reception 8am-midnight; ⊜⊗; ⓊWarschauer Strasse, ⓈWarschauer Strasse) is a great spot for a drink. Sit on the sun deck in summer.

o For farm-fresh organic meals, report to the restaurant (p154) at the Michelberger hotel.

A **B** **C** **D**

Palisadenstr

23
1

Karl-Marx-Allee

Volkspark
Friedrichshain

Auerstr

Weidenweg

Computerspielemuseum
6

17

Weberwiese

Karl-Marx-Allee

2 Singerstr

Rüdersdorfer Str

Strasse der Pariser Kommune

Koppenstr

Franz-
Mehring-Platz

Marchlewskistr

Gubener Str

Kadiner Str

Wedekindstr

Rüdersdorfer Str

Corneliusplatz

3 **26**

Wriezener Karree

Warschauer Str

Ostbahnhof

Ostbahnhof

An der Ostbahn

Am Ostbahnhof

Strasse der Pariser Kommune

Helsingforser Str

FRIEDRICHSHAIN

Stralauer
Platz **3**

4
Holzmarkt
14

Helen-Ernst-Str

Helsingforser
Platz

Urban
Spree
5

Mühlenstr

Mildred-Harnack-Str

Mercedes-
Benz Arena

Hedwig-Wachenheim-Str

Tamara-Danz-Str

Warschauer
Str.

20

5

East Side
Gallery

13

Warschauer
Str

Warschauer Platz

Rudolfstr

Rotherstr

Köpenicker Str

Spree River

Mühlenstr

Ehrenbergstr

6

Schlesisches
Tor

Oberbaumbrücke

Stralauer Allee

Oberbaumbrücke

A **B** **C** **D**

Petersburger Str

Bänschstr

Rigaer Str

Prostauer Str

Frankfurter Tor
U
Karl- Marx- Allee
2

Frankfurter Allee

U Samariterstr

Warschauer Str

Niederbarnimstr

Mainzer Str

15

Boxhagener Str
16
8

Scharnweberstr

Grünberger Str

Simon-Dach-Str

Gabriel-Max-Str

Gärtnerstr

Boxhagener Platz
25 4
22

Weichselstr

Traveplatz

Kopernikusstr
7
9
Wühlischstr

Krossener Str

Jessnerstr
Weserstr

21 12

Seumestr

Simplonstr

RAW Gelände
11
18
Revaler Str

Sonntagstr

10

24

Lenbachstr

Neue Bahnhofstr

Markstrasse

Rudolfplatz

Modersohnstr

Weichselstr

Simplonstr

Corinthstr

Markgrafendamm

Ostkreuz
S
19

N 0 400 m
0 0.2 miles

E F G H
1 2 3 4 5 6

Sights

Volkspark Friedrichshain PARK

1 ◉ MAP P148, B1

Berlin's oldest public park has provided relief from urbanity since 1840 but has been hilly only since the late 1940s, when wartime debris was piled up here to create two 'mountains' – the taller one, **Mont Klamott**, rises 78m high. Diversions include expansive lawns for lazing, tennis courts, a half-pipe for skaters, a couple of handily placed beer gardens and an outdoor cinema. (btwn Am Friedrichshain, Friedenstrasse, Danziger Strasse & Landsberger Allee; ⏱24hr; 🚌142, 200, 🚊M5, M6, M8, M10)

Karl-Marx-Allee STREET

2 ◉ MAP P148, E2

It's easy to feel like Gulliver in the Land of Brobdingnag when walking down monumental Karl-Marx-Allee, one of Berlin's most impressive GDR-era relics. Built between 1952 and 1960, the 90m-wide boulevard runs for 2.3km between Alexanderplatz and Frankfurter Tor and is a fabulous showcase of East German architecture. A considerable source of national pride back then, it provided modern flats for comrades and served as a backdrop for military parades. (admission free; Ⓤ Strausberger Platz, Weberwiese, Frankfurter Tor)

Holzmarkt AREA

3 ◉ MAP P148, A4

The Holzmarkt urban village on the Spree is a perpetually evolving creative campus that beautifully embodies Berlin's visionary spirit. Drop by to poke around buildings handcrafted from wood and recycled materials, dance in the world's smallest disco, and watch the boats on parade with a cold beer from the on-site brewery or while tucking into gourmet food at trashy-arty Katerschmaus (p154). (www.holzmarkt.com; Holzmarktstrasse 25; Ⓤ Jannowitzbrücke)

Boxhagener Platz SQUARE

4 ◉ MAP P148, F3

The heart of Friedrichshain, 'Boxi' is a lovely, leafy square with benches and a playground. It's framed by restored 19th-century buildings harbouring trend-conscious cafes, artisanal shops, bakeries and fair-fashion boutiques. The area is busiest during the Saturday **farmers market** (⏱9am-3.30pm Sat) and on Sunday, when a flea market (p157) brings in folks from all over town. (⏱24hr; Ⓟ; 🚌240, Ⓢ Warschauer Strasse, Ⓤ Samariterstrasse, Warschauer Strasse)

Urban Spree ARTS CENTRE

5 ◉ MAP P148, D4

Keep tabs on the latest trends in urban culture at this grassroots arts space in the RAW Gelände (p156) compound. Comprising a gallery, a bookshop, artist studios and a

The Stasi: When the Walls Had Ears

Founded in 1950 and modelled after the Soviet KGB, East Germany's *Ministerium für Staatssicherheit* (Ministry of State Security, 'Stasi' for short) was secret police, central intelligence agency and bureau of criminal investigation all rolled into one. It put millions of its own citizens under surveillance in order to suppress internal opposition and, by 1989, had 91,000 official full-time employees and 189,000 IMs (*inoffizielle Mitarbeiter*, unofficial informants). The latter were regular folks recruited to spy on their coworkers, friends, family and neighbours.

Stasi Museum

The **Stasimuseum** (Map p148; ☏030-553 6854; www.stasimuseum.de; Haus 1, Normannenstrasse 20; adult/concession €8/6, tour additional €2; ⊙10am-6pm Mon-Fri, 11am-6pm Sat & Sun, English tours 3pm Mon, Thu & Sat; Ⓤ Magdalenenstrasse) inside the actual former Stasi ministry in Lichtenberg, just east of Friedrichshain, dissects the structure, methods, impact and all-pervasive power of the Stasi. The often cunningly low-tech surveillance devices (hidden in watering cans, rocks, even neckties) are among the most intriguing exhibits. Another highlight are the stuffy original offices, private quarters and conference rooms of Erich Mielke, head of the Stasi from 1957 until the end. Information panels are partly in English. There's also a van with teensy, lightless cells that was used to transport suspects to the nearby Stasi prison.

Stasi Prison

Officially called **Gedenkstätte Berlin-Hohenschönhausen** (☏030-9860 8230; www.stiftung-hsh.de; Genslerstrasse 66; tours adult/concession €6/3, exhibit free; ⊙tours in English 11.45am, 2.15pm & 3.45pm, more frequent German tours 10am-4pm, exhibit 9am-6pm; Ⓟ; ⛟M5), the Stasi prison is, if anything, even creepier than the Stasi Museum. Tours, sometimes led by former inmates, reveal the full extent of the terror and cruelty perpetrated upon thousands of suspected political opponents, many utterly innocent. If you've seen the Academy Award–winning film *The Lives of Others*, you may recognise many of the original settings. An exhibit uses photographs, objects and a free audioguide to document both the daily life of those behind bars and of the Stasi staff.

concert room, it's especially fun in summer when the beer garden and street-food container units open and an eclectic line-up of festivals keeps revellers coming back.

The building's facade doubles as an 'Artist Wall', with new urban artworks going up every month or so. (📞030-7407 8597; www.urbanspree.com; Revaler Strasse 99; 🕐gallery & bookshop 2-7pm Wed-Fri, noon-7pm Sat & Sun Nov-Mar, to 6pm Apr-Oct; 🚊M10, Ⓤ Warschauer Strasse, Ⓢ Warschauer Strasse)

Computerspiele-museum
MUSEUM

6 ◎ MAP P148, B1

No matter if you grew up with Nimrod, Pac-Man, World of Warcraft or no games at all, this well-curated museum takes you on a fascinating trip down computer-game memory lane while putting the industry's evolution into historical and cultural context. Colourful and engaging, it features interactive stations amid some 300 original exhibits, including an ultra-rare 1972 Pong arcade machine and its twisted modern cousin, the 'PainStation'. (Computer Games Museum; 📞030-6098 8577; www.computerspielemuseum.de; Karl-Marx-Allee 93a; adult/concession €9/6; 🕐10am-8pm; Ⓤ Weberwiese)

Eating

1990 Vegan Living
VEGAN €

7 🍴 MAP P148, F4

Serving a vibrant range of small and large bowls, this family-run Vietnamese joint channels the unassuming, buzzy vibe of the streets of Hanoi. Inside you'll be embraced by an array of imported knick-knacks, while outside tables give you a full-on view of the Boxhagener Platz action. (📞030-8561 4761; www.restaurant-1990.de; Krossener Strasse 19; small plates €4.20, mains €9.90; 🕐noon-10.30pm Mon-Sat, 1-10.30pm Sun; 🛜🪑; 🚊M10, M13, Ⓤ Samariterstrasse, Warschauer Strasse)

Hako Ramen am Boxi JAPANESE €

8 🍴 MAP P148, F3

This cosy ramen spot is full of authentic Japanese flair and the wafting smell of rich broths. Sit at the bar or grab a table to enjoy a warming, savoury noodle bowl based on pork, chicken or vegan broth. (📞030-8442 6700; www.hakoramen.com; Boxhagener Strasse 26; mains €9-12; 🕐noon-10pm; 🪑; 🚊M10, 21, Ⓤ Samariterstrasse)

Silo Coffee
CAFE €

9 🍴 MAP P148, F4

If you've greeted the day with bloodshot eyes, get back in gear at this Aussie-run coffee and brunch joint favoured by Friedrichshain's hip and international crowds. Beans from local Fjord Coffee Roasters ensure possibly the best flat white in town, while sourdough from Sironi (Markthalle Neun) adds scrumptiousness to the poached-egg avo toast. (www.silo-coffee.com; Gabriel-Max-Strasse 4; dishes €6-12; 🕐9.30am-3.30pm Mon-Fri, to 5pm Sat & Sun; 🛜🪑; 🚊M10, M13, Ⓤ Warschauer Strasse, Ⓢ Warschauer Strasse)

Vöner
VEGAN €

10 🍴 MAP P148, H5

Vöner stands for 'vegan doner kebab' and is a spit-roasted blend of wheat protein, vegetables, soy meal, herbs and spices. It was dreamed up more than 20 years ago by Holger Frerichs, a one-time resident of a so-called *Wagen-burg*, a countercultural commune made up of old vans, buses and caravans. The alt-spirit lives on in his original Vöner outlet. (www. voener.de; Boxhagener Strasse 56; dishes €3.50-6.50; ⏰2-7pm Sun-Fri, noon-10pm Sat; 🖋; Ⓢ Ostkreuz)

Khwan
THAI, BARBECUE €€

11 🍴 MAP P148, E4

For some of the best northern Thai barbecue this side of Chiang Mai,

pounce on this rustic warehouse ensconced – for now – among the clubs and bars on the RAW Gelände (p156) strip. Your senses will be hooked by the aromatic smoke (*khwan* in Thai) wafting from the wood-fire pit, where flames lick chicken, pork, fish and vegetables to succulent perfection. (📞0152 5902 1331; http://khwan berlin.com; RAW Gelände, Revaler Strasse 99; plates €6-23; ⏰6-11.30pm Wed-Sat, 11am-3pm & 5-10.30pm Sun; 🛜; 🚊M10, M13, Ⓤ Warschauer Strasse, Ⓢ Warschauer Strasse)

Spätzle & Knödel
GERMAN €€

12 🍴 MAP P148, F4

This elbows-on-the-table gastro-pub provides a southern German comfort-food fix, including roast pork with dark-beer gravy, goulash

Computerspiele-museum

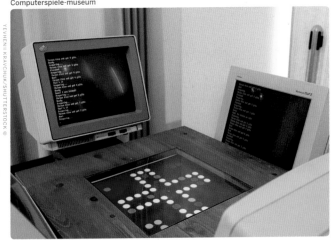

YEVHENII KRAVCHUK/SHUTTERSTOCK ©

with red cabbage and, of course, the eponymous *Spaetzle* (German mac 'n' cheese) and *Knödel* (dumplings). Bonus: Bavarian Riegele, Maisel and Weihenstephan beers on tap. (☑030-2757 1151; www. spaetzleknoedel.de; Wühlischstrasse 20; mains €9-16; ⊙4-10pm Mon-Fri, 3-10pm Sat & Sun; Ⓤ Samariterstrasse)

Michelberger INTERNATIONAL €€€

13 MAP P148, C5

Ensconced in one of Berlin's coolest **hotels** (d from €105; Ⓟ 🐾 🛜), Michelberger makes creative dinners from whatever its local organic farmers, hunters and foragers have supplied that day. Both vegans and omnivores can be accommodated. Sit inside the lofty, white-tiled restaurant or in the breezy courtyard. (☑030-2977 8590; www.michelberger hotel.com; Warschauer Strasse 39; dinner tasting menu €32; ⊙8am-1pm & 6-10pm; 🛜 🧋; Ⓢ Warschauer Strasse, Ⓤ Warschauer Strasse)

Katerschmaus EUROPEAN €€€

14 MAP P148, A4

This kitty (*Kater* is a male cat in German) is sleek and rustic-chic and hides out riverside in a carefully designed ramshackle space on the Holzmarkt (p150) cultural playground. It inclines towards ingredients from regional suppliers and will have you purring for its wicked crème brûlée. (☑0152 2941 3262; www.katerschmaus.de; Holzmarktstrasse 25; mains €21-45; ⊙1-11pm Tue-Sat; 🛜; Ⓤ Jannowitzbrücke, Ⓢ Jannowitzbrücke)

Drinking

Tentación BAR

15 MAP P148, G3

Resisting temptation can be tough. Forget about it when visiting Tentación (Spanish for 'temptation'); its main ammo is the Latin American cult spirit mezcal, which reportedly has psychedelic qualities. The tiny parlour dispenses a huge selection of the wicked potion along with Mala Vida, the owner-brewed craft beer. A small menu of feisty Oaxacan munchies is on stand-by for the peckish. (☑030-2393 0401; www.tentacionmezcalothek.de; Scharnweberstrasse 32; ⊙5-11pm Wed-Sat, noon-8pm Sun; Ⓤ Samariterstrasse)

Zeroliq BAR

16 MAP P148, F3

Keep your brain clear and sensitise your taste buds by sipping cocktails sans alcohol at aptly named Zeroliq. Aside from serving nearly three dozen booze-free craft beers, it also pours de-alcoholised wines and vegan mocktails that won't make you miss the real thing. Try the Summer in Berlin or the Zeroligroni. (☑0157 9237 4581; www.zeroliq.com; Boxhagener Strasse 104; ⊙5pm-midnight Thu-Sat; Ⓤ Samariterstrasse)

Briefmarken Weine WINE BAR

17 MAP P148, C1

For *dolce vita* right on socialistera Karl-Marx-Allee, head to this charmingly nostalgic Italian wine bar ensconced in a former stamp shop. The original wooden cabinets cradle a hand-picked selection of Italian bottles that complement a snack menu of yummy cheeses, prosciutto and salami, plus a pasta dish of the day. Best to book ahead. (📞030-4202 5292; www. briefmarkenweine.eu; Karl-Marx-Allee 99; ⏰7pm-midnight Mon & Wed-Sat, 5pm-midnight Tue; Ⓤ Weberwiese)

Cassiopeia
CLUB

18 🚇 MAP P148, E4

No wild dance-a-thons during the pandemic, but this delightfully trashy venue is trying to keep alive by only hosting corona-compatible events such as quiz nights and spoken-word sessions, and beaming others (DJ sets and concerts) straight to you via livestream. (www.cassiopeia-berlin.de; Gate 2, RAW Gelände, Revaler Strasse 99; ⏰from 7pm or later Tue-Sun; 🚊M10, M13, Ⓤ Warschauer Strasse, Ⓢ Warschauer Strasse)

Krass Böser Wolf
BAR

19 🚇 MAP P148, H6

Although the name translates roughly as 'very mean wolf', this dimly lit lair is actually a friendly imbibing spot. Pop by to wind down the day with a cold beer from the tap or rev things up a notch with one of the classic or original cocktails. (📞0157 3966 2585; www.krassboeserwolf.de; Markgrafendamm 36; ⏰6pm-3am Mon-Sat; Ⓢ Ostkreuz)

Monster Ronson's Ichiban Karaoke
KARAOKE

20 🚇 MAP P148, D5

Knock back a couple of brewskis if you need to loosen your nerves before belting out your best Adele or Lady Gaga at this mad, great karaoke joint. Shy types can book a private booth for music and mischief. (📞030-8975 1327; www. karaokemonster.de; Warschauer Strasse 34; ⏰7-11pm Tue, Thu & Fri, 2-11pm Sat & Sun; Ⓢ Warschauer Strasse, Ⓤ Warschauer Strasse)

Hops & Barley
MICROBREWERY

21 🚇 MAP P148, F4

Conversation flows as freely as the unfiltered pilsner, malty *Dunkel* (dark) and fruity *Weizen* (wheat) produced right here at one of Berlin's oldest craft breweries (since 2008). The pub is inside a former butcher's shop and still has the tiled walls to prove it. For variety, the brewmeisters also produce weekly blackboard specials and potent unfiltered cider. (📞030-2936 7534; www.hopsandbarley-berlin.de; Wühlischstrasse 22/23; ⏰5pm-late Mon-Fri, from 3pm Sat & Sun; 🚊M13, Ⓤ Warschauer Strasse, Ⓢ Warschauer Strasse)

Entertainment

The Wall Comedy Club
COMEDY

22 ⭐ MAP P148, F3

Hosts an eclectic roster of English-language stand-up comedy showcases every night, featuring

Urban Playground

The jumble of derelict buildings called **RAW Gelände** (Map p148, E4; Revaler Strasse 99; admission free; S Warschauer Strasse, Ostkreuz, U Warschauer Strasse) is one of the last subcultural bastions in central Berlin. Founded in 1867 as a train repair station ('*Reichsbahn-Ausbesserungs-Werk*', aka RAW), it remained in operation until 1994. Since 1999 the graffiti-slathered grounds have been a thriving offbeat sociocultural centre for creatives of all stripes. They also harbour clubs, bars, a beer garden, an indoor skate park, a 'beach' club, a bunker-turned-climbing-wall and a Sunday flea market.

Changes are underfoot, however, as the land was bought by an investor in 2015 and the district government green-lit its partial development in 2019, albeit with the proviso that 10% of the area must continue to be set aside for sociocultural ventures.

international touring talent as well as some funny German comics. If you dare, sign up for Tuesday's open-mic night. (www.thewallcomedy.com; Grünberger Strasse 84; 7pm-1am Mon-Wed, to 3am Thu-Sat; M13, U Samariterstrasse)

Kino International   CINEMA

 23 MAP P148, A1

The East German film elite once held its movie premieres in this 1960s cinema, whose glamorous array of chandeliers and glitter curtains is a show in itself. Today it presents smartly curated international indie hit flicks daily, usually in the original language with German subtitles.

The panorama bar is great for pre- or post-screening libations. The Monday 10pm time slot is reserved for gay-themed movies.

(030-2475 6011; www.yorck.de; Karl-Marx-Allee 33; tickets €7.50-10; U Schillingstrasse)

Shopping

Loveco   FASHION & ACCESSORIES

24 MAP P148, G5

Lovable Loveco gets a big eco-nod of approval for its huge selection of vegan, sustainable and fair-trade clothing and accessories by local and international labels such as Armed Angels, People Tree and LovJoi. All pieces are handpicked by owner Christina and beautifully presented in the stylish store with its signature swing.

See the website for locations of branches in Kreuzberg and Schöneberg. (www.loveco-shop.de; Sonntagstrasse 29; noon-10pm Mon-Fri, 11am-7pm Sat; S Ostkreuz)

BOX HARD STUDIOS/SHUTTERSTOCK ©

Grosser Antikmarkt Ostbahnhof

Flohmarkt Boxhagener Platz
MARKET

25 🔒 MAP P148, F3

Wrapped around leafy Boxhagener Platz, this fun flea market is just a java whiff away from oodles of convivial cafes. Although the presence of pro vendors has grown, there are still plenty of regular folks here to unload their spring-cleaning detritus at bargain prices. (Boxhagener Platz; ⏰10am-6pm Sun; 🚋M13, Ⓢ Warschauer Strasse, Ⓤ Warschauer Strasse, Samariterstrasse)

Grosser Antikmarkt Ostbahnhof
ANTIQUES

26 🔒 MAP P148, A3

If you're after antiques and collectables, head to this sprawling market outside the Ostbahnhof's north exit. Up to 150 vendors hawk yesteryear's collectables. Forage for old coins, Iron Curtain–era relics, gramophone records, books, stamps, jewellery and bric-a-brac, but don't expect clothing or recent knick-knacks. (Erich-Steinfurth-Strasse; ⏰9am-5pm Sun; Ⓢ Ostbahnhof)

Explore ◈

Prenzlauer Berg

Splendidly well-groomed Prenzlauer Berg is one of Berlin's most charismatic residential neighbourhoods, filled with cafes, historic buildings and indie boutiques. On Sundays, the world descends on its Mauerpark for flea marketeering, karaoke and chilling. A visit here is easily combined with the Gedenkstätte Berliner Mauer (p94), a 1.4km-long exhibit that illustrates how the Berlin Wall shaped the city.

The Short List

○ **Mauerpark (p160)** *Spending a sunny Sunday digging for flea-market treasures and cheering on karaoke crooners in this popular park reclaimed from a section of the Berlin Wall death strip.*

○ **Kulturbrauerei (p164)** *Catching a concert, movie or street-food market at this venerable red-brick brewery-turned-cultural centre.*

○ **Kollwitzplatz (p164)** *Taking a leisurely ramble around this leafy square and its side streets lined with beautiful townhouses, convivial cafes and indie boutiques.*

Getting There & Around

Ⓤ The U2 stops at Schönhauser Allee, Eberswalder Strasse and Senefelderplatz.

🚋 The M1 links Museumsinsel and Prenzlauer Berg via the Scheunenviertel, Kastanienallee and Schönhauser Allee. The M13 heads to Friedrichshain.

Ⓢ Schönhauser Allee is the most useful station on the S41 and S42 Ringbahn (Circle Line).

Neighbourhood Map on p162

Walking Tour 🥾

Sundays Around the Mauerpark

Locals, expats and tourists – everyone flocks to the Mauerpark on Sunday. Doubled in size in 2020, it's an energetic urban tapestry where a flea market, karaoke and bands provide entertainment, and people gather for barbecues, basketball and boules. A graffiti-covered section of the Berlin Wall recalls the time when the park was part of the death strip separating East and West Berlin.

Walk Facts

Start Oderberger Strasse; Ⓤ Eberswalder Strasse

End Northern Mauerpark; Ⓤ Schönhauser Allee

Length 1.7km; one hour without stops

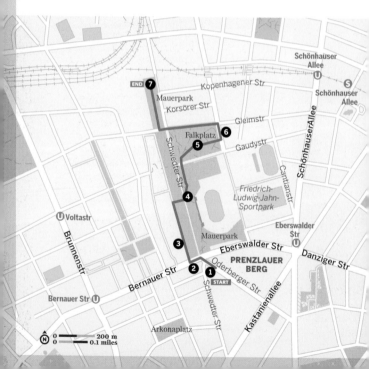

❶ Bright Beginnings

Start on Oderberger Strasse, which is lined with restaurants and cafes, including **Bonanza Coffee Heroes** (www.bonanzacoffee.de; Oderberger Strasse 35; ◷8.30am-7pm Mon-Fri, 10am-7pm Sat & Sun; 🛜). Look up at the beautiful facades of the restored 19th-century townhouses that were saved from demolition in the late '70s when the street dead-ended at the Berlin Wall.

❷ Confronting Cold War History

During the Cold War, East met West at Bernauer Strasse, now paralleled by a 1.4km-long linear multimedia memorial exhibit (p94) that vividly illustrates the realities of life with the Berlin Wall. Its eastern terminus is here at Schwedter Strasse. Even walking just a short stretch west offers eye-opening insights.

❸ Urban Archaeology

Hit the **Flohmarkt im Mauerpark** (www.flohmarktimmauerpark.de; Bernauer Strasse 63-64; ◷9am-6pm Sun) for some quality hunting and gathering of retro threads, cool stuff by local designers and vintage vinyl. Afterwards, fortify yourself at a street-food stall or listen to the buskers in the park.

❹ Bearpit Karaoke

On most summer Sundays, Berlin's best free entertainment kicks off around 3pm when Joe Hatchiban sets up his custom-made mobile karaoke unit in the Mauerpark's amphitheatre. Join the crowds in cheering and clapping for eager crooners ranging from giggling 11-year-olds to Broadway-calibre belters.

❺ Falkplatz

Studded with ancient chestnut, oak, birch, ash and poplar trees, this leafy park was a parade ground for Prussian soldiers back in the 19th century and was used to grow vegetables right after WWII. Today, you can watch kids frolicking around the sea-lion fountain.

❻ Burgermania

New York meets Berlin at expat favourite **Bird** (📞030-5105 3283; www.thebirdinberlin.com; Am Falkplatz 5; burgers €10-14.50, steaks from €22.50; ◷6-10pm Mon-Thu, 4-11pm Fri, noon-11pm Sat, noon-10pm Sun; 🛜), whose dry-aged steaks, burgers and hand-cut fries might just justify the hype. Sink your teeth into a dripping half-pounder trapped between a toasted English muffin.

❼ Northern Mauerpark

To escape the Mauerpark frenzy and see where the locals relax, head north of the Gleimstrasse tunnel. This is where you'll find an enchanting birch grove, a farm playground complete with barn-yard animals, and a climbing wall.

Prenzlauer Berg

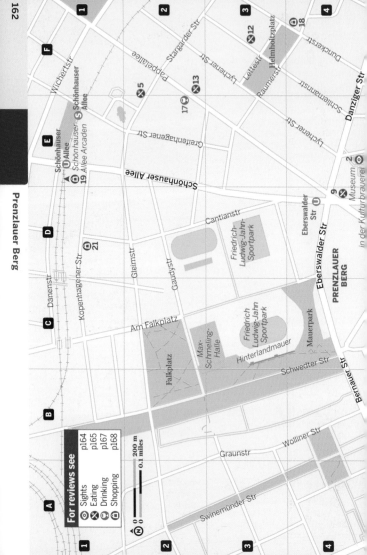

For reviews see

⊚ Sights	p164
✗ Eating	p165
🍸 Drinking	p167
🛍 Shopping	p168

200 m
0.1 miles

Wichertstr

Schönhauser
Ⓤ Allee

Schönhauser
Ⓢ Schönhauser
Allee
Allee

19 Allee Arcaden

Pappelallee

Stargarder Str

✗5

17 🍸

✗13

Lychener Str

✗12

Leitestr

Helmholtzplatz

18 🍸

Dunckerstr

Schliemannstr

Danziger Str

Lychener Str

Raumerstr

Greifenhagener Str

Schönhauser Allee

Eberswalder
Str

9 ✗

Museum 2
in der Kulturbrauerei

PRENZLAUER
BERG

Eberswalder Str

Cantianstr

Friedrich-
Ludwig-Jahn-
Sportpark

Kopenhagener Str

Danenstr

Gleimstr

21 🛍

Gaudystr

Am Falkplatz

Falkplatz

Max-
Schmeling-
Halle

Friedrich
Ludwig-Jahn
Sportpark

Hinterlandmauer

Mauerpark

Schwedter Str

Bernauer Str

Wolliner Str

Graunstr

Swinemünder Str

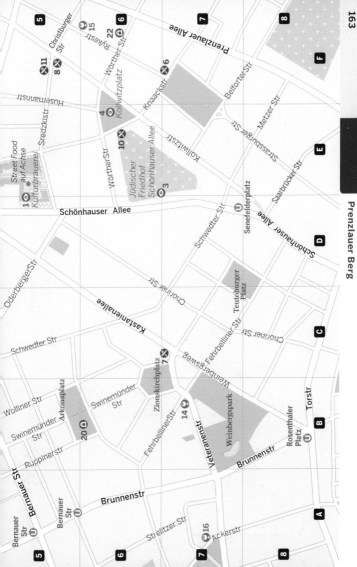

Christburger Str

Prenzlauer Allee

Husemannstr

Sredzkistr

Street Food auf Achse
Kulturbrauerei

Wörther Str

Kollwitzplatz

Knaackstr

Schönhauser Allee

Jüdischer
Friedhof

Wörther Str

Kollwitzstr

Belforter Str

Metzer Str

Strassburger Str

Saarbrücker Str

Schönhauser Allee

Senefelderplatz

Schönhauser Allee

Oderberger Str

Schwedter Str

Choriner Str

Kastanienallee

Teutoburger
Platz

Choriner Str

Fehrbelliner Str

Weinbergsweg

Schwedter Str

Schwedter Str

Schwedter Str

Wolliner Str

Arkonaplatz

Swinemünder Str

Swinemünder Str

Ruppiner Str

Zionskirchplatz

Fehrbelliner Str

Veteranenstr

Weinbergspark

Brunnenstr

Rosenthaler
Platz

Torstr

Bernauer
Str

Bernauer Str

Bernauer Str

Brunnenstr

Strelitzer Str

Ackerstr

Sights

Kulturbrauerei
CULTURAL CENTRE

1 ◉ MAP P162, D5

The fanciful red-and-yellow brick buildings of this 19th-century brewery have been upcycled into a cultural powerhouse with a small village's worth of venues, from concert and theatre halls to nightclubs, dance studios, a multiplex cinema and a free GDR-history museum. The main entrances are on Knaackstrasse and Sredzkistrasse. (☎030-4435 2170; www.kulturbrauerei.de; btwn Schönhauser Allee, Knaackstrasse, Eberswalder Strasse & Sredzkistrasse; Ⓟ; ⓂM1, ⓊEberswalder Strasse)

Museum in der Kulturbrauerei
MUSEUM

2 ◉ MAP P162, E4

Original documents, historical footage and objects (including a camper-style Trabi car) illustrate daily life under socialism in East Germany in themed rooms in this government-curated exhibit. As you wander the halls, you'll realise the stark contrast between the lofty aspirations of the socialist state and the sobering realities of material shortages, surveillance and oppression its people had to endure. (☎030-467 777 911; www.hdg.de; Knaackstrasse 97; admission free; ⊙9am-6pm Tue-Fri, 10am-6pm Sat & Sun; Ⓟ; ⓂM1, M10, 12, ⓊEberswalder Strasse)

Jüdischer Friedhof Schönhauser Allee
CEMETERY

3 ◉ MAP P162, E6

Berlin's second Jewish cemetery opened in 1827 and hosts some 25,000 dearly departed, including the artist Max Liebermann and the composer Giacomo Meyerbeer. It's a pretty place with dappled light filtering through big old chestnuts and linden trees and a sense of melancholy emanating from ivy-draped graves and toppled tombstones. The nicest and oldest have been moved to the Lapidarium by the main entrance. (☎030-441 9824; www.jg-berlin.org; Schönhauser Allee 22; ⊙8am-4pm Mon-Thu, 7.30am-1pm Fri; ⓊSenefelderplatz)

Kollwitzplatz
SQUARE

4 ◉ MAP P162, E6

OK, so it's triangular, but Kollwitzplatz is still the prettiest square in Prenzlauer Berg. The leafy park in its centre is tot heaven, with three playgrounds plus a bronze sculpture of the artist Käthe Kollwitz, who used to live nearby. Cafes and restaurants invite lingering, but for the full-on local vibe, swing by the **farmers markets** (⊙noon-7pm Thu Apr-Dec, to 6pm Thu Jan-Mar, 9am-4pm Sat) on Thursday and Saturday. (🚹; ⓊSenefelderplatz)

Eating

Eispatisserie Hokey Pokey

ICE CREAM €

5  MAP P162, F2

The debate over Berlin's best ice cream may have local foodies in a headlock, but there's no doubt that Hokey Pokey is a strong contender. People brave rock-star-worthy lines to get their fix of these creamy orbs of goodness created by a master patissier with a knack for adventurous new flavour combos. (☎0176 8010 3080; www. hokey-pokey.de; Stargarder Strasse 72; ⊙noon-10pm May-Sep, changes seasonally; 🚋M1, Ⓤ Schönhauser Allee, Ⓢ Schönhauser Allee)

Umami

VIETNAMESE €

6  MAP P162, F7

A mellow 1950s lounge vibe and an inspired menu of Indochine home cooking divided into 'regular' and 'vegetarian' choices are the main draws at this restaurant with an expansive sidewalk terrace. Leave room for its cupcake riff (called 'popcake'). The six-course family meal is a steal at €23 for two, plus €10 per additional person. (☎030-2886 0626; www.umami-restaurant. de; Knaackstrasse 16; most mains €7.80; ⊙noon-11pm; 🛜 🖉; 🚋M2, Ⓤ Senefelderplatz)

W-Der Imbiss

FUSION €

7  MAP P162, C7

The self-described home of 'indo-mexi-cal-ital' fusion, W is always

Kulturbrauerei

EZDAN/SHUTTERSTOCK ©

Street Food auf Achse

On Sundays, the Kulturbrauerei (p164) gets mobbed by hungry folk keen on a first-class culinary journey at economy prices. Dozens of mobile kitchens set up for **Street Food auf Achse** (Map p162, E5; www. streetfoodaufachse.de; ⏱noon-6pm Sun late Jan–mid-Nov) in the courtyard of the cultural complex, and there's a beer garden as well as occasional live music and other entertainment.

busy as a beehive with fans of its signature naan pizza freshly baked in the tandoor oven and decorated with anything from avocado to smoked salmon. Other standouts are the fish tacos, the thali curry spread and the tandoori salmon. (☏030-4435 2206; www.w-derimbiss. de; Kastanienallee 49; dishes €5-20; ⏱noon-10pm Sun-Thu, to 11pm Fri & Sat; ☏; ☐M1, ⓤRosenthaler Platz)

Anna Blume CAFE €

 8 MAP P162, F5

Potent java, tantalising cakes, weekly-changing hot dishes, and flowers from the attached shop perfume the art-nouveau interior of this corner cafe named for a 1919 Dadaist poem by German artist Kurt Schwitters. In fine weather the terrace offers primo people-watching. Great for breakfast (served any time), especially if

you order the tiered tray for two. (☏030-4404 8749; www.cafe-anna-blume.de; Kollwitzstrasse 83; breakfast €4-13, mains €8-15; ⏱9am-midnight; ☐M2, M10, ⓤEberswalder Strasse)

Konnopke's Imbiss GERMAN €

9 MAP P162, D4

Brave the inevitable queue at this famous sausage kitchen, ensconced in the same spot below the U-Bahn viaduct since 1930, but now equipped with a heated pavilion, an English menu and a vegan sausage option. The 'secret' tomato sauce topping its *Currywurst* comes in a five-tier heat scale from mild to wild. (☏030-442 7765; www. konnopke-imbiss.de; Schönhauser Allee 44a; sausages €1.80-3.50; ⏱11am-6pm Mon-Fri, noon-6pm Sat; ☏; ☐M1, M10, M13, ⓤEberswalder Strasse)

Der Blaue Fuchs GEORGIAN €€

10 MAP P162, E6

In a soft-toned ambience accented by hand-painted 1920s wallpaper and GDR-era lamps, you can feast on such Georgian palate teasers as *gebjalia* (pesto-filled mozzarella rolls) or the richly nuanced *chakapuli* (veal stew). Just be careful not to fill up on the classic – and highly addictive – *khachapuri* (cheese-filled bread). There's a kids' play corner. (☏030-2607 4244; https:// derblauefuchs.metro.bar; Knaackstrasse 43; mains €11-19.50; ⏱4-11pm Tue-Thu, noon-11pm Fri-Sun; ☝; ⓤSenefelderplatz)

Chutnify INDIAN €€

11 MAP P162, F5

Aparna Aurora's haunt spices up Berlin's bland Indian-food scene with adroitly spiced South Indian street food. Her specialities are dosas (a type of savoury rice-lentil crêpe) filled with flavour-packed curries and stews, but it's well worth exploring what's behind such lesser-known dishes as *vada* and *idli*. (☏030-4401 0795; www.chutnify.com; Sredzkistrasse 43; mains €10-17; ⏱noon-3pm & 6-10pm Tue-Fri, noon-10pm Sat & Sun; ⚲; ⛊M2, M10, ⓊEberswalder Strasse)

Kanaan MIDDLE EASTERN €€

12 MAP P162, F3

In this feel-good venture, an Israeli biz whiz and a Palestinian chef have teamed up to bring a progressive blend of vegan and vegetarian Middle Eastern street fare to Berlin. The hummus is divine, especially when pimped up with garlic-lemon sauce and marinated vegetables. (☏01590 134 8077; www.kanaan-berlin.de; Schliemannstrasse 15; mains lunch & brunch €4-15, dinner €20; ⏱6-10pm Wed & Thu, noon-10pm Fri-Sun; ⚲; ⛊M1, ⓊSchönhauser Allee, ⓈSchönhauser Allee)

Mrs Robinson's INTERNATIONAL €€€

13 MAP P162, F2

When Ben Zviel and Samina Raza launched their minimalist casual fine-dining parlour (white-brick walls, polished wooden tables) in 2016, they immediately garnered the attention of the local culinary cognoscenti. Treating sustainably sourced seasonal and local fare with respect and time-tested techniques, their intensely flavoured dishes beautifully capture the city's adventurous and experimental spirit. Only natural wines feature on the wine list. (☏030-5462 2839; www.mrsrobinsons.de; Pappelallee 29; 4-/5-/6-course menu €62/65/75; ⏱6-11pm Thu-Mon; ⚲; ⛊12, ⓊEberswalder Strasse)

Drinking

Weinerei Forum WINE BAR

14 MAP P162, B7

Serving homemade cakes and light meals by day, this living-room-style cafe turns into a wine bar after 8pm. It works on the honour principle: you 'rent' a wine glass for €2, then taste as much vino as you like and in the end decide what you want to pay. Please be fair to keep

Water Tower Cafe Scene

Mere steps from Kollwitzplatz, a lively cafe and restaurant scene has sprung up in a sunny spot below Berlin's oldest water tower (1877), a round red-brick landmark that is now honeycombed with pie-sliced flats. Now looking prim and pretty, its engine room (since demolished) served as one of Germany's first improvised concentration camps in 1933.

this fantastic concept going. (www.weinerei.com; Fehrbelliner Strasse 57; ⊙10am-midnight; 📶; 🚊M1, 12, ⓊRosenthaler Platz)

Bryk Bar
COCKTAIL BAR

15 🚇 MAP P162, F6

Both vintage and industrial elements contribute to the unhurried, dapper ambience at this darkly lit cocktail lab. Bar chef Frank Grosser whips unusual ingredients into such experimental liquid teasers as the rum-based Kamasutra with a Hangover that's topped with white-chocolate-horseradish foam. The free dill popcorn is positively addictive. (📞030-2246 8055; www.bryk-bar.com; Rykestrasse 18; ⊙4pm-late; 🚊M2, M10, 🚇Prenzlauer Allee)

BrewDog
CRAFT BEER

16 🚇 MAP P162, A7

Scottish cult beer-maker BrewDog now brings its fine suds to Berlin. Its modern-industrial flagship with brick walls and dark wood has some 30 taps dispensing its own draughts (try the Punk IPA) alongside a rotating roster of German and global guest pours. The pizza (€10 to €12) pairs well with the amber fluid. (📞030-4847 7770; www.brewdog.com; Ackerstrasse 29; ⊙noon-midnight Sun-Thu, to 2am Fri & Sat; 🚊12, M5, M8, ⓊBernauer Strasse)

Becketts Kopf
COCKTAIL BAR

17 🚇 MAP P162, E2

Past Samuel Beckett's portrait, the art of cocktail-making is taken very seriously. Since 2004, the husband-and-wife owners have constantly upped the mixology ante by giving special twists to classic cocktails and by whipping up idiosyncratic concoctions that truly stimulate all the senses. Most of the spirits they use come from small suppliers. (📞030-4403 5880; www.becketts-kopf.de; Pappelallee 64; ⊙7pm-2am; 🚊12, Ⓢ Schönhauser Allee, ⓊSchönhauser Allee)

Shopping

Goldhahn und Sampson
FOOD

18 🔒 MAP P162, F4

Harissa paste, additive-free red miso and crusty German bread are among the global pantry stockers at this stylish gourmet gallery. Owners Sascha and Andreas travel the world to source all items, most of them rare, organic and from small artisanal suppliers. For inspiration, nose around the cookbook library or join up for a class at the on-site cooking school. (📞030-4119 8366; www.goldhahnundsampson.de; Dunckerstrasse 9; ⊙8am-8pm Mon-Fri, 9am-8pm Sat; 🚊12, ⓊEberswalder Strasse)

DearGoods
FASHION & ACCESSORIES

19 🔒 MAP P162

DearGoods was Germany's first all-vegan fashion boutique when it opened in 2012. It now has branches in other cities but remains uncompromisingly married to its original concept. Shop with a clear conscience for threads and accessories made from eco-friendly organic materials that will have you looking – and feeling – great. (030-9838 9926; www.deargoods. com; Schivelbeiner Strasse 35; 11am-8pm Mon-Fri, to 6pm Sat; Schönhauser Allee)

Trödelmarkt Arkonaplatz

MARKET

20 MAP P162, B6

Surrounded by cafes perfect for carbo-loading, this smallish flea market on a leafy square lets you ride the retro frenzy with plenty of groovy furniture, accessories, clothing, vinyl and books, including some East German vintage items. It's easily combined with a visit to the famous Flohmarkt im Mauerpark (p161). (www.troedelmarkt-arkonaplatz. de; Arkonaplatz; 10am-4pm Sun; M1, M10, Bernauer Strasse)

Sugafari

FOOD

21 MAP P162, D1

Take a trip around the world one candy at a time in this happiness-inducing cornucopia of sugary treats. No matter whether you're a homesick expat, nostalgic for your favourite childhood sweets or curious about Ma Hwa Cookies from China or a Bon Bon Bum lollie from Colombia, you'll find it in this sweet little shop or its online store. (030-9560 9713; www.sugafari.com; Kopenhagener Strasse 69; 2-7.30pm Tue-Fri, 11am-6pm Sat; M1, Schönhauser Allee, S Schönhauser Allee)

Saint Georges English Bookshop

BOOKS

22 MAP P162, F6

Laid-back and low-key, Saint Georges bookshop is a sterling spot to track down new and used English-language fiction and non-fiction. The selection includes plenty of rare and out-of-print books as well as a big shelf of literature by German and international authors translated into English. (030-8179 8333; www.saintgeorges bookshop.com; Wörther Strasse 27; 11am-8pm Mon-Fri, to 7pm Sat; M2, Senefelderplatz)

Worth a Trip 👓

Discover Schloss & Park Sanssouci

This glorious park-and-palace ensemble is what happens when a king has good taste, plenty of cash and access to the finest architects and artists of the day. Sanssouci was dreamed up by Frederick the Great (1712–86) and is anchored by the eponymous palace, built as a summer retreat in Potsdam, a quick train ride from Berlin. His great-greatnephew Friedrich Wilhelm IV (1795–1861) added a few more buildings. Unesco gave the entire complex World Heritage status in 1990.

📞 0331-969 4200

www.spsg.de

Maulbeerallee

day pass to all palaces
adult/concession €19/14

🕐 varies by palace

🚌 614, 650, 692, 695, 697

Schloss Sanssouci

The biggest stunner, and what everyone comes to see, is **Schloss Sanssouci** (adult/concession incl tour or audioguide €14/10; ⏱ 10am-5.30pm Tue-Sun Apr-Oct, to 4.30pm Nov-Mar), Frederick the Great's famous summer palace. Designed by Georg Wenzeslaus von Knobelsdorff in 1747, the rococo gem sits daintily above vine-draped terraces with the king's grave nearby.

Standouts on the tour (guided or self-guided) include the **Konzertsaal** (Concert Hall), whimsically decorated with vines, grapes and even a cobweb where sculpted spiders frolic. The king himself gave flute recitals here. Also note the intimate **Bibliothek** (library), lidded by a gilded sunburst ceiling, where the king would seek solace amid 2000 leather-bound tomes ranging from Greek poetry to the latest releases by his friend Voltaire. Another highlight is the **Marmorsaal** (Marble Room), an elegant white Carrara-marble symphony modelled after the Pantheon in Rome.

Chinesisches Haus

The adorable **Chinese House** (Am Grünen Gitter; adult/concession €4/3; ⏱ 10am-5.30pm Tue-Sun May-Oct) is among the park's most photographed buildings thanks to its enchanting exterior of exotically dressed, gilded figures shown sipping tea, dancing and playing musical instruments amid palm-shaped pillars. Inside is a precious porcelain collection.

Bildergalerie

The **Picture Gallery** (pictured; Gallery of Old Masters; Im Park Sanssouci 4; adult/concession €6/5; ⏱ 10am-5.30pm Tue-Sun May-Oct) shelters Frederick the Great's prized collection of old masters, including such pearls as Caravaggio's *Doubting Thomas,* Anthony van Dyck's *Pentecost* and several works by Peter Paul Rubens. Behind the rather plain facade hides a

★ Top Tips

○ Book your timed ticket to Schloss Sanssouci online to avoid wait times and/ or disappointment.

○ Avoid visiting on Monday when most palaces are closed.

○ The sanssouci+ ticket, a one-day pass to palaces in Potsdam, costs €19 (concession €14).

✗ Take a Break

○ Right in the park, **Drachenhaus** (☏ 0331-505 3808; www.drachenhaus.de; Maulbeerallee 4; mains €10-23; ⏱ 11am-7pm daily Apr-Oct, noon-6pm Tue-Sun Nov, Dec & Mar, noon-6pm Sat & Sun Jan & Feb; ♿; ☒ 695) serves coffee, cakes and seasonal cuisine.

★ Getting There

Potsdam is 24km southwest of the city centre.

☒ It's 25 minutes from Berlin Hauptbahnhof or Zoologischer Garten to Potsdam Hauptbahnhof by RE1 trains.

Ⓢ The S7 takes 40 minutes.

sumptuous arrangement of gilded ornamentation, yellow and white marble and a patterned stone floor that is perhaps just as impressive as the mostly large-scale paintings that cover practically every inch of wall space.

Neues Palais

The final palace commissioned by Frederick the Great, the **Neues Palais** (New Palace; Am Neuen Palais; adult/concession incl tour or audioguide €6/5; ◷10am-5.30pm Tue-Sun Apr-Oct, 10am-4.30pm Wed-Mon Nov-Mar) has made-to-impress dimensions, a central dome and a lavish exterior capped with a parade of sandstone figures. After extensive restoration, most of the building's highlights are once again accessible, including the shell-festooned **Grottensaal** (Grotto

Hall) festival hall and the magnificent **Marmorsaal** (Marble Hall), where visitors walk across a raised pathway to protect the precious marble floor illuminated by eight massive crystal chandeliers. Also looking splendid is the redone **Unteres Fürsten-quartier** (Lower Royal Suite), which consists of a concert room, an oval-shaped chamber, an antechamber and, most impressively, a dining room with walls sheathed in red silk damask with gold-braided trim.

Orangerieschloss

Modelled after an Italian Renaissance villa, the 300m-long, 1864-built **Orangery Palace** (An der Orangerie 3-5; adult/concession €6/5, tower €3/2; ◷10am-5.30pm Tue-Sun May-Oct, 10am-5.30pm Sat & Sun Apr) was the favourite building project of Friedrich

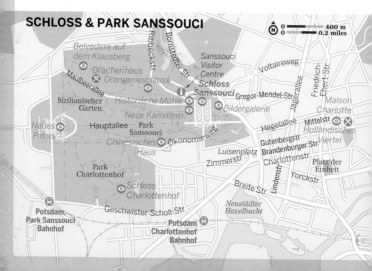

SCHLOSS & PARK SANSSOUCI

Wilhelm IV – a passionate Italophile. Its highlight is the **Raffaelsaal** (Raphael Hall), which brims with 19th-century copies of the famous painter's masterpieces.

Neue Kammern

The **New Chambers** (Park Sanssouci; adult/concession incl tour or audioguide €6/5; ◷10am-5.30pm Tue-Sun Apr-Oct), built by Knobelsdorff in 1748, were originally an orangery and later converted into a guest palace. The interior drips with rococo opulence, most notably the square **Jasper Hall**, which is drenched in precious stones and lidded by a Venus fresco, and the **Ovidsaal**, a grand ballroom with gilded wall reliefs depicting scenes from Ovid's *Metamorphosis*.

Schloss Charlottenhof

This small **palace** (Charlottenhof Palace; Geschwister-Scholl-Strasse 34a; tours adult/concession €6/5; ◷tours 10am-5.30pm Tue-Sun May-Oct) started out as a baroque country manor before being expanded by Karl Friedrich Schinkel for Friedrich Wilhelm IV in the late 1820s. The building is modelled on classical Roman villas and features a Doric portico and a bronze fountain.

Historische Mühle

This reconstructed 18th-century Dutch-style **windmill** (Historic Windmill; ☏0331-550 6851; Maulbeerallee 5; adult/concession €4/3; ◷10am-6pm Apr-Oct) contains exhibits about the history of the mill and mill technology, and offers a close-up look at the grinding mechanism and a top-floor viewing platform.

Nearby: Museum Barberini

The original **Barberini Palace** (☏0331-236 014 499; www.museum-barberini.com; Alter Markt, Humboldtstrasse 5-6; adult weekday/weekend €16/18, concession/under 18yr daily €10/free; ◷10am-7pm Wed-Mon, 1st Thu of month to 9pm, last entry 1hr before closing; 🚌605, 614, 631, 🚊91, 92, 93, 96, 98 Alter Markt/Landtag) was a baroque Roman palazzo commissioned by Frederick the Great and bombed to bits in WWII. Since January 2017, a majestic replica houses a private art museum that mounts several high-calibre exhibits per year with an artistic arc that spans East German works, old masters and modern greats such as Gerhard Richter.

Survival Guide

U-bahn on the Oberbaum bridge PHOTOCRED MICHAL BEDNAREK/SHUTTERSTOCK ©

Before You Go

Book Your Stay

o Berlin has over 143,000 hotel rooms but the most desirable properties book up quickly, especially in summer and around major holidays, festivals and trade shows; prices soar and reservations are essential during these periods.

o Otherwise, rates are mercifully low by Western capital standards. Options range from luxurious ports of call to ho-hum international chains, trendy designer boutique hotels to Old Berlin–style B&Bs, happening hostels to handy self-catering apartments.

o The most central district is Mitte. Hotels around Kurfürstendamm are plentiful but put you a *U-Bahn* ride away from most blockbuster sights and nightlife.

o Lodging in Kreuzberg and Friedrichshain is handy for party animals.

o Berlin's hostel scene is as vibrant as ever with

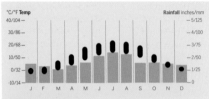

When to Go

Winter (Nov–Feb)
Cold and dark, snow possible. Sights are crowd-free; theatre and concert season in full swing.

Spring (Mar–May)
Mild, often sunny. Sights start getting busier; festival season kicks off; beer gardens and outdoor cafes open.

Summer (Jun–Aug)
Warm to hot, often sunny; thunderstorms possible. Peak tourist season; sights and museums are super-busy; life moves outdoors.

Autumn (Sep & Oct)
Mild, often sunny. Theatre, concert and football (soccer) seasons start up.

dorms beds available for as little as €10.

Useful Websites

Lonely Planet (lonely planet.com/germany/berlin/hotels) Lonely Planet's online booking service with insider low-down on the best places to stay.

Visit Berlin (www.visitberlin.de) Official Berlin tourist office; books rooms at partner hotels with a best-price guarantee.

Boutique Hotels Berlin

(www.boutiquehotels-berlin.com) Booking service for about 20 hand-picked boutique hotels.

Berlin30 (www.berlin30.com) Online low-cost booking agency for hotels, hostels, apartments and B&Bs in Berlin.

Best Budget

Grand Hostel Berlin Classic (www.grand hostel-berlin.de) Connect to the magic of yesteryear at this historic lair imbued with both character and modern amenities.

EastSeven Berlin Hostel (www.east seven.de) Friendly and low-key hostel with communal vibe ideal for solo travellers.

Circus Hostel (www. circus-berlin.de) This Berlin classic is a superb launch pad for fun-seekers and culture cravers.

Hostel One80° (www. one80hostels.com) Vast next-gen hostel with hotel-style comforts and amenities.

Best Midrange

Orania (www.orania. berlin) Culturally minded style pad with superb restaurant and live concerts.

Adina Apartment Hotel Berlin Checkpoint Charlie (www. adinahotels.com) Ideal base for budget-conscious, space-craving self-caterers.

Michelberger Hotel (www.michelberger hotel.com) Zeitgeist-capturing crash pad with funky industrial DIY aesthetics and popular restaurant.

25hours Hotel Bikini Berlin (www.25hours-hotels.com) Inner-city playground with easy access to top shopping and rooms overlooking Zoo Berlin.

Almodóvar Hotel (www.almodovarhotel. de) Solid eco-cred pairs with mod-cons and rooftop sauna.

Best Top End

Hotel am Steinplatz (www.hotelsteinplatz. com) Reincarnated art-deco jewel with top-notch bar and restaurant.

Hotel de Rome (www. roccofortehotels.com) Posh player in a former bank building with rooftop bar and bank-vault spa.

S/O Berlin Das Stue (www.das-stue.com) Charismatic refuge from the urban bustle with understated grandeur and the Tiergarten park as a front yard.

Hotel Adlon Kempinski (www.kempinski. com) First opened in 1907, this is Berlin's most high-profile defender of the grand tradition.

City Tax

Value-added tax (VAT; 7%) has long been included in room rates, but since 1 January 2014 an additional 5% 'city tax' is added to the net room rates (ie excluding VAT and fees for amenities and services. Business travellers are exempt from this tax).

Arriving in Berlin

Berlin Brandenburg Airport

○ After an eight-year delay, Berlin Brandenburg Airport (BER), about 27km south of the city centre, launched its inaugural flight on 31 October 2020.

○ BER consists of Terminal 1 (T1) and Terminal 2 (T2). Only T1 will be open initially.

○ The railway station is below Terminal 1

and served by the FEX Airport Express, regional trains and the S-Bahn.

o The FEX Airport Express travels every half hour between 4am and midnight to/from the Hauptbahnhof (main train station) to T1/2 in 30 minutes. Also stops at Gesundbrunnen and Ostkreuz.

o Regular Deutsche Bahn trains designated RE7 and RB14 make hourly trips from the city centre to T1/T2 (30 minutes).

o The S9 leaves every 20 minutes and takes about 45 minutes to/from the city centre.

o You'll need an ABC ticket (€3.80) for all journeys.

o Cabs to central Berlin take about an hour and cost around €60.

Hauptbahnhof

o Berlin's central train station is just north of the Reichstag and Brandenburg Gate and is served by the U-Bahn, the S-Bahn, trams and buses.

o Taxis and public transport leave from outside the north exit (Europaplatz).

o Lockers are located behind the Reisebank currency exchange on level OG1 between platforms 14 and 15.

Zentraler Omnibusbahnhof

o The **Zentraler Omnibusbahnhof** (ZOB, Central Bus Station; 📞 030-3010 0175; www.zob-berlin.de; Messedamm 8; **S** Messe Nord/ICC, **U** Kaiserdamm) is near the trade fairgrounds on the western city edge. Flixbus also stops at around a dozen other points in town, including the BER airport and Alexanderplatz.

o The closest U-Bahn station to ZOB is Kaiserdamm, about 400m north and served by the U2 line, which travels through the city centre. Tickets cost €2.90 (Tariff AB).

o The nearest S-Bahn station is Messe Süd/ICC, about 400m southeast of ZOB. It is served by the Ringbahn (circle line) S41/S42 and handy for such districts as Prenzlauer Berg, Friedrichshain and Neukölln. You'll need an AB ticket (€3).

o Budget about €15 for

a taxi ride to the western city centre around Zoo station and €28 to the eastern city centre around Alexanderplatz.

Getting Around

U-Bahn

o The U-Bahn is the quickest way of getting around Berlin.

o Lines (referred to as U1, U2 etc) operate from 4am until about 12.30am and throughout the night on Friday, Saturday and public holidays (all lines except the U4).

o From Sunday to Thursday, night buses take over in the interim.

S-Bahn

o S-Bahn trains (S1, S2 etc) don't run as frequently as the U-Bahn, but they make fewer stops and are thus useful for covering longer distances.

o Trains operate from 4am to 12.30am and all night on Friday, Saturday and public holidays.

Tickets & Passes

o One ticket is valid for all forms of public transport.

o The network comprises fare zones A, B and C with tickets available for zones AB, BC or ABC.

o AB tickets, valid for two hours, cover most city trips (interruptions and transfers allowed, but round trips are not). Exceptions: Potsdam and BER (ABC tariff).

o Children aged six to 14 qualify for reduced (ermässigt) rates; kids under six travel free.

o Buy tickets from vending machines at U- or S-Bahn stations, aboard trams, at station offices or at news kiosks sporting the yellow BVG logo. Vending machines accept credit cards; tram vending machines only take cash. Bus drivers have suspended selling tickets during the COVID-19 pandemic.

o Single tickets, except those bought in trams, must be validated at station platform entrances.

o On-the-spot fine for travelling without a valid ticket: €60.

o A range of travel passes offer better value than single tickets.

Bus

o Buses run frequently between 4.30am and 12.30am.

o Night buses (N19, N23 etc) take over after 12.30am.

o MetroBuses, designated M19, M41 etc, operate 24/7.

Tram

o Trams (Strassenbahn) operate almost exclusively in the eastern districts.

o Trams, designated M1, M2 etc, run 24/7.

Bicycle

o Bicycles may be taken aboard designated U-Bahn and S-Bahn carriages (look for the bicycle symbol) as well as night bus lines N1 to N9 (Sunday to Thursday only) and trams.

o You need a separate FahrradTicket (€2.10, 24-hour-ticket €5).

Taxi

o You can order a **taxi** (📞030-210 101, 030-443 322, 030-210 202; www.taxi-in-berlin.de) by phone or by app (eg Free Now,

Taxi Berlin, www.taxi.eu), flag one down or pick one up at a rank. At night, cars often wait outside theatres, clubs and other venues.

o Flag fall is €3.90, then it's €2.30 per kilometre up to 7km and €1.65 for each additional kilometre.

o Tip about 10%.

o The Kurzstreckentarif (short-trip rate) lets you ride in a cab for up to 2km for €6 provided you flag down a moving taxi and request this rate before boarding.

Essential Information

Accessible Travel

o The Visit Berlin tourist board publishes an excellent accessibility online guide at www.visitberlin.de/en/accessible-berlin (also in English).

o Access ramps and/or lifts are available in many public buildings, including train stations and museums.

o Most buses, trains and trams are wheelchair-accessible and many U-Bahn and S-Bahn stations are equipped with ramps or lifts. For trip-planning assistance, contact the **BVG** (☎030-194 49; www.bvg.de).

Business Hours

The following are typical opening hours, although these may vary seasonally and by location (city centre or the suburbs).

Bars 5pm–1am or later

Boutiques 11am–7pm Monday–Friday, to 5pm or 6pm Saturday

Cafes 8am–8pm

Clubs 11pm–5am or later

Restaurants 11am–11pm

Shops 10am–8pm Monday–Saturday

Supermarkets 8am–8pm or later; some 24 hours

Discount Cards

Berlin Welcome Card (www.berlin-welcome card.de) Valid for un-limited public transport for one adult and up to three children under 14; up to 50% discount to 200 sights, attractions and tours; available for up to six days.

CityTourCard (www.citytourcard.com) Similar to the Berlin Welcome Card but a bit cheaper and with fewer discounts.

Museumspass Berlin (adult/concession €29/14.50) Buys admission to the permanent exhibits of about 30 museums for three consecutive days. Sold at tourist offices and participating museums.

Electricity

Type C
220V/50Hz

Late-Night & Sunday Shopping

o One handy feature of Berlin culture is the *Spätkauf* (*Späti* in local vernacular), which are small neighbourhood stores stocked with the basics and open from early evening until 2am or later.

o Some supermarkets stay open until midnight; a few are open 24 hours.

o Shops in major train stations (eg Hauptbahnhof, Friedrichstrasse, Ostbahnhof) are open late and on Sunday.

Emergencies

Ambulance	📞112
Fire department	📞112
Germany's country code	📞49
International access code	📞00
Police	📞110

Money

o ATMs (*Geldautomat*) are the best and easiest way to get cash. Most are accessible 24/7.

o Credit cards are accepted by most retailers, hotels, restaurants, bars, taxi drivers, venues and public-transport vending machines.

o Always carry some cash for smaller purchases and in case plastic is not accepted.

Public Holidays

Shops, banks and public and private offices are closed on the following nationwide *gesetzliche Feiertage* (public holidays):

Neujahrstag (New Year's Day) 1 January

Internationaler Frauentag (International Women's Day) 8 March

Ostern (Easter) March/ April; Good Friday, Easter Sunday and Easter Monday

Christi Himmelfahrt (Ascension Day) Forty days after Easter, always on a Thursday

Maifeiertag (Labour Day) 1 May

Pfingsten (Whitsun/ Pentecost Sunday and Monday) May/June

Tag der Deutschen Einheit (Day of German Unity) 3 October

Weihnachtstag (Christmas Day) 25 December

Zweiter Weihnachtstag (Boxing Day) 26 December

Telephone Services

o Berlin's city code is 📞030; Germany's country code is 📞49.

o Mobile phones operate on GSM900/1800.

o Local SIM cards can be used in unlocked European and Australian phones and are sold at supermarkets, convenience stores and electronics shops for as little as €5.

o US multiband phones also work in Germany.

Tourist Information

Visit Berlin (www. visitberlin.de), the Berlin tourist board, operates five walk-in offices, info desks at the airports, and a **call centre** (📞030-2500 2333; ⏰9am-6pm Mon-Fri) whose multilingual staff field general questions and make hotel and ticket bookings.

Berlin Brandenburg Airport (📞030-250 025; www.visitberlin.de; Terminal 1, Level 0; ⏰9am-4pm; 🚆Flughafen BER Terminal 1-2, Ⓢ Flughafen BER Terminal 1-2)

Brandenburger Tor (📞030-250 023; www. visitberlin.de; Pariser Platz, Brandenburger Tor, south wing; ⏰10am-7pm Apr-Aug, to 6pm Sep-Mar; Ⓢ Brandenburger Tor, Ⓤ Brandenburger Tor)

Hauptbahnhof (📞030-250 025; www. visitberlin.de; Hauptbahnhof, Europaplatz entrance, ground fl; ⏰8am-8pm; Ⓢ Hauptbahnhof, 🚆Hauptbahnhof)

Visas

o EU nationals need only their national identity card or passport to enter Germany.

○ Citizens of Australia, Canada, Israel, Japan, New Zealand, Switzerland and the US are among those who need only a valid passport (no visa) if entering as tourists for a stay of up to three months within a six-month period.

○ Passports must be valid for at least another three months beyond the planned departure date.

○ Nationals from other countries need a Schengen visa to enter Germany. Check with a German consulate in your country.

Responsible Travel

Overtourism

○ Travel off-season: avoid the summer months (May–Sep) and Easter, and opt for mid-week instead of weekends.

○ Expand your sightseeing to Berlin's outer districts and discover such gems as a horseshoe-shaped Bauhaus complex, a Renaissance military fortress or a bucolic Chinese garden.

Dos & Don'ts

○ Do say 'Guten Tag' when entering a business.

○ Do state your last name at the start of a phone call.

○ Do bring a small gift or flowers when invited to a home-cooked meal.

○ Bring a bag to shop at supermarkets and pack your own groceries.

○ Don't be late for appointments and dinner invitations.

○ Check ahead to see whether you can pay by credit card, especially when eating out.

○ Peruse the bilingual GoLocal magazine produced by the local tourism authority Visit Berlin. (www.visitberlin.de/system/files/document/visitBerlin_Going-Local-Magazin_Vol2_1.11_DS_0.pdf) or download the GoLocal app)

○ Stay more than a couple of days and take the train to crystal-clear lakes, a romantically ruined monastery, nature preserves or World War II battlefields in the surrounding Brandenburg countryside.

Support Local & Give Back

○ Frequent organic, sustainable, vegan, vegetarian or zero-waste cafes and restaurants.

○ Before booking accommodation, check if a property follows sustainable hospitality standards.

○ Look into volunteering opportunities with Give Something Back to Berlin (https://gsbtb.org)

Leave a Light Footprint

○ Ditch the plane or car and travel by train or coach instead – Berlin is well-served from throughout Europe.

○ Berlin has a brilliant public transport system. Use it!

○ You'll find bike and e-scooter rental schemes throughout the city. Or rent a kayak and explore Berlin by water.

Language

It's easy to pronounce German because almost all sounds are also found in English – just read our pronunciation guides as if they were English and you'll be understood.

In German, word stress falls mostly on the first syllable – in our pronunciation guides the stressed syllable is indicated with italics.

Note that German has polite and informal forms for 'you' (*Sie* and *du* respectively). When addressing people you don't know well, use the polite form. In this language guide, polite forms are used, unless you see (pol/inf) which indicates we've given both options. Also note that (m/f) indicates masculine and feminine forms.

To enhance your trip with a phrasebook, visit **lonelyplanet.com**.

Basics

Hello.
Guten Tag.   goo·ten taak

Goodbye.
Auf   owf
Wiedersehen.   vee·der·zey·en

How are you? (pol/inf)
Wie geht es   vee gayt es
Ihnen/dir?   ee·nen/deer

Fine, thanks.
Danke, gut.   dang·ke goot

Please.
Bitte.   bi·te

Thank you.
Danke.   dang·ke

Excuse me.
Entschuldigung.   ent·shul·di·gung

Sorry.
Entschuldigung.   ent·shul·di·gung

Yes./No.
Ja./Nein.   yah/nain

Do you speak (English)?
Sprechen Sie   shpre·khen zee
Englisch?   eng·lish

I (don't) understand.
Ich verstehe   ikh fer·shtay·e
(nicht).   (nikht)

Eating & Drinking

I'm a vegetarian. (m/f)
Ich bin Vegetarier/   ikh bin ve·ge·
   tah·ri·er/
Vegetarierin.   ve·ge·*tah*·ri·e·in

Cheers!
Prost!   prawst

That was delicious!
Das war sehr   das vahr zair
lecker.   le·ker

Please bring the bill.
Die Rechnung,   dee rekh·nung
bitte.   bi·te

I'd like ...
Ich möchte ...   ikh *merkh*·te ...

a coffee   *einen Kaffee*   ai·nen ka·fay

a glass of   *ein Glas*   ain glas
wine   *Wein*   wain

a table   *einen Tisch*   ai·nen tish
for two   *für zwei*   für tsvai
   Personen   per·*zaw*·nen

two beers   *zwei Bier*   tsvai beer

Shopping

I'd like to buy ...
Ich möchte ...   ikh *merkh*·te ...
kaufen.   kow·fen

May I look at it?
Können Sie es   ker·nen zee es
mir zeigen?   meer tsai·gen

How much is it?
Wie viel kostet das?   vee feel kos·tet das

That's too expensive.
Das ist zu teuer. das ist tsoo *toy*·er

Can you lower the price?
Können Sie mit ker·nen zee mit
dem Preis dem prais
heruntergehen? he·*run*·ter·gay·en

There's a mistake in the bill.
Da ist ein Fehler in dah ist ain *fay*·ler in
der Rechnung. dair *rekh*·nung

Emergencies

Help!
Hilfe! *hil*·fe

Call a doctor!
Rufen Sie roo·fen zee
einen Arzt! ai·nen artst

Call the police!
Rufen Sie roo·fen zee
die Polizei! dee po·li·*tsai*

I'm lost.
Ich habe ikh *hah*·be
mich verirrt. mikh fer·*irt*

I'm ill.
Ich bin krank. ikh bin krangk

Where's the toilet?
Wo ist die Toilette? vo ist dee to·a·*le*·te

Time & Numbers

What time is it?
Wie spät ist es? vee shpayt ist es

It's (10) o'clock.
Es ist (zehn) Uhr. es ist (tsayn) oor

morning	*Morgen*	*mor*·gen
afternoon	*Nach-mittag*	*nahkh*·mi·tahk
evening	*Abend*	*ah*·bent
yesterday	*gestern*	*ges*·tern
today	*heute*	*hoy*·te
tomorrow	*morgen*	*mor*·gen

1	*eins*	ains
2	*zwei*	tsvai
3	*drei*	drai
4	*vier*	feer
5	*fünf*	fünf
6	*sechs*	zeks
7	*sieben*	zee·ben
8	*acht*	akht
9	*neun*	noyn
10	*zehn*	tsayn
100	*hundert*	*hun*·dert
1000	*tausend*	*tow*·sent

Transport & Directions

Where's ...?
Wo ist ...? vaw ist ...

What's the address?
Wie ist die vee ist dee
Adresse? a·*dre*·se

Can you show me (on the map)?
Können Sie es mir ker·nen zee es meer
(auf der Karte) (owf dair *kar*·te)
zeigen? *tsai*·gen

I want to go to ...
Ich mochte ikh *merkh*·te
nach ... fahren. nahkh ... *fah*·ren

What time does it leave?
Wann fährt es ab? van fairt es ap

What time does it arrive?
Wann kommt van komt
es an? es an

Does it stop at ...?
Hält es in ...? helt es in ...

I want to get off here.
Ich mochte hier ikh *merkh*·te heer
aussteigen. ows·*shtai*·gen

Behind the Scenes

Send Us Your Feedback

We love to hear from travellers – your comments help make our books better. We read every word, and we guarantee that your feedback goes straight to the authors. Visit **lonelyplanet.com/contact** to submit your updates and suggestions.

Note: We may edit, reproduce and incorporate your comments in Lonely Planet products such as guidebooks, websites and digital products, so let us know if you don't want your comments reproduced or your name acknowledged. For a copy of our privacy policy visit lonelyplanet.com/privacy.

Andrea's Thanks

A big heartfelt thanks to the following wonderful people who have plied me tips, insight, information, ideas and encouragement in researching this book (in no particular order): Henrik Tidefjärd, Barbara Woolsey, Kerstin Riedel, Claudia Scheffler, Frank Engster, Heiner and Claudia Schuster, Anna Lübbe, Renate Freiling, Shachar and Dorit Elkanati, Bernd Olsson, Friederike Werner and, of course, David Peevers.

Acknowledgements

Cover photograph: Berlin cityscape, 21AERIALS/Shutterstock ©

Back photograph: Ampelmann street crossing icon, Michael Major/Shutterstock ©

Photographs pp34–5 (from left): fhm/Getty Images ©; Westend61/Getty Images ©; Svetlana Turchenick/Shutterstock ©; Linka A Odom/Getty Images ©; Stavros Argyropoulos/Shutterstock ©

This Book

This 7th edition of Lonely Planet's *Pocket Berlin* guidebook was researched and written by Andrea Schulte-Peevers, who also wrote the previous two editions. This guidebook was produced by the following:

Senior Product Editor
Sandie Kestell

Cartographers
Hunor Csutoros, Mark Griffiths

Product Editors
Grace Dobell, Amy Lynch

Book Designers
Norma Brewer, Gwen Cotter

Assisting Editors
Janet Austin, Sarah Bailey, Michelle Bennett, Monique Perrin, Martine Power

Assisting Cartographer
Julie Dodkins

Cover Researcher
Gwen Cotter

Thanks to Daniel Bolger, Sonia Kapoor, Kate Kiely, Kirsten Rawlings

Index

See also separate subindexes for:

🍴 **Eating p188**

🍷 **Drinking p189**

🎭 **Entertainment p190**

🛍 **Shopping p190**

Our Writer

Andrea Schulte-Peevers

Born and raised in Germany and educated in London and at UCLA, Andrea has travelled the distance to the moon and back in her visits to some 75 countries. She has earned her living as a professional travel writer for over two decades, and authored or contributed to nearly 100 Lonely Planet titles, as well as writing for newspapers, magazines and websites around the world. She also works as a travel consultant, translator and editor. Andrea's destination expertise is especially strong when it comes to Germany, Dubai and the UAE, Crete and the Caribbean Islands. She makes her home in Berlin.

Published by Lonely Planet Global Limited
CRN 554153
7th edition – Feb 2022
ISBN 978 1 78868 074 5
© Lonely Planet 2022   Photographs © as indicated 2022
10 9 8 7 6 5 4 3 2 1
Printed in Malaysia

Although the authors and Lonely Planet have taken all reasonable care in preparing this book, we make no warranty about the accuracy or completeness of its content and, to the maximum extent permitted, disclaim all liability arising from its use.

All rights reserved. No part of this publication may be copied, stored in a retrieval system, or transmitted in any form by any means, electronic, mechanical, recording or otherwise, except brief extracts for the purpose of review, and no part of this publication may be sold or hired, without the written permission of the publisher. Lonely Planet and the Lonely Planet logo are trademarks of Lonely Planet and are registered in the US Patent and Trademark Office and in other countries. Lonely Planet does not allow its name or logo to be appropriated by commercial establishments, such as retailers, restaurants or hotels. Please let us know of any misuses: lonelyplanet.com/ip.